In SYMphony AUS

David J. Broadhead

Dec 1989.

In SYMPHONY AUSTERE

RICHARD FRERE

ILLUSTRATION bY ERIC Ritchie

BALNAIN BOOKS

Printed in Scotland by Pillans and Wilson Specialist Litho Printers Ltd,
Edinburgh.
Colour separation by C.M.R. Graphics, East Kilbride.
Binding by Hunter and Foulis, Edinburgh.
Handwritten titles by John Callum (Lettercraft), Dornoch.
Design by Simon Fraser.
Design Consultant: Sarah Fraser.

Originally published under the title of *Thoughts of a Mountaineer*, by Oliver
and Boyd (Edinburgh) in 1952, this new edition is a complete revision of the
earlier text.

The publishers would like to acknowledge with gratitude The Scottish Arts
Council for their financial assistance in the publication of this volume.

Published in 1989
by Balnain Books
Druim House, Lochloy Road,
Nairn IV12 5LF
Scotland

Distributors:
Bookspeed
48a Hamilton Place,
Edinburgh EH3 5AX
tel: (031) 225 4950

ISBN 0–9509792–8–7

CONTENTS

Dedication—To my mother and father, who gallantly sacrificed their peace of mind that I might go free upon the hills.

*t*here are few writers, aspiring or established, who can say firmly with Pontius Pilate, "What I have written, I have written" and admit no wish or need to change. Most of us like to alter our typescripts at least once, and often as many as ten times, before we doubtfully return the proofs to our editors, thus burning our bridges.

Eventually the book appears in the shops. After a decent interval we read it again. In my case, surely not unique, I find that I would like to alter every word and improve every phrase. But it is too late: a wonderful opportunity has been missed. It is pointless to cry over split infinitives. One is painfully reminded of Fitzgerald's quatrain, aimed at the newly-published:

The Moving Finger writes; and having writ
Moves on: nor all thy Piety nor Wit
Shall lure it back to cancel half a line
Nor all thy Tears wash out a word of it.

Imagine then my pleasure when Balnain Books offered to reprint my first book and gave me *carte blanche* to make any changes I thought fit. This pipe-dream had lingered in my head since 1952 when an Edinburgh firm published my brain-child under the title of *Thoughts of a Mountaineer*. My wish had been to call it *In Symphony Austere*, felicitous words from a poem of Wordsworth, and to illustrate it with drawings by a sympathetic artist. My publishers thought otherwise, imposed their own title and preferred photographs.

Now, most happily, this situation is reversed. The original title is in favour and the book is embellished by Eric Ritchie's strong and thought-provoking drawings. As to the text, this revival has given me the chance to bleach out some of its more purple passages and to simplify to some extent a succession of esoteric images which arose in a teenage mind quite devoid of discipline or order.

Richard Frere 1989

A Song
at the Dawn

tHe prEludE

he farmhouse at Mid Lairgs is given over to ruin. Rot and decay are its only inmates. Sometimes a sheep may poke its face inside the broken door or a tramp seek shelter here to spend a lonely night with the darkness and, perhaps, his dreams of plenty. Besides these, nobody comes.

The wind may shake the hanging plaster on the walls or cry uneasily in the glassless window-frames. The drip-drip of rain might sound in the stone-floored kitchen. Perhaps there will be the banging of a door, but otherwise there will be no sound.

The mountain ash that stands beside the house renews its life with the revolving year, but for the old house there is no renewal. Life has been here and life has gone, sounds without echoes. Does the spirit of the house remember?

Yet six years ago boys came here, boys with their dreams, their contrivances and their joy. Windows were patched up and the deep dust swept from the floors. It was a brief flash in a long darkness. Then the dust fell again, slowly; the wind punched the glass from the windows; the shy tramp came back. The boys had gone to try their teeth upon the hard nut of War.

Jimmy and I found it first on a November evening—a squat bulk, darker than the surrounding moorland, younger than the hills yet far more lonely. We had come over the pass from Moy, *en route* for Inverness, following the cart track that had once been a military road. We rested, in the deep twilight, on the hump of a Wade bridge and thought of the workmanship that had so stoutly resisted two hundred years of rain, frost and storm. From here we saw the house.

Curiosity led us to the door, which resisted us. I was turning away when the padlock which Jimmy was rattling came apart in his hands. "It wants us in," he said, a remark out of character for he was not much given to whimsy. We entered, exchanging twilight for the gloom of the sepulchre. We could only sense where the windows were. Beneath our feet we could feel the floorboards sagging.

"Let's get out of here," I said, "it's dangerous—and pretty spooky as well!" By the time we were a hundred yards away the house had vanished into the moor.

A few months later I came across the house again, this time with my friend Kenneth. By then it was early Spring and the hills behind the house were still beautiful with snow. We went round to the door and found the padlock just where it had fallen. We toured the downstairs rooms and climbed a rickety staircase to a pair of attics. Everywhere dust burdened the window sills and excluded the light and from the ceilings cobwebs hung, heavy as stalactites. In the kitchen there was a monstrous range, the kind of thing that breaks the housewife's heart. By it lay a small, broken perambulator, looking as if it had beeen cast there in a moment of pique years before. The only other objects in the room were a triangular stool and a long drinking trough.

Finding nothing to interest us we went outside and sat down on the grass. We took out some sandwiches from a rucksack and munched them in silence. We were enjoying a gentle day.

"Shall we go to Bheurlaich?" asked Kenneth, referring to the highest mountain within reach, a mere mile away and some sixteen hundred feet high.

"Okay," I said, "may as well. Beat you to the top of the pass." We broke into a run, not stopping until we had reached the swell of the hillside. Kenneth, having got his breath back, remarked:

"It would make a great place to climb from."

"What!" I said, "That old ruin? And where'd we climb? Bheurlaich is okay for an evening stroll, but that's about all. Now, if we could move it to the Cairngorms, then you'd be talking."

"You miss the point" said Kenneth, "I mean it would be good for the odd weekend, roughing it, keeping in form. I think it'd be nice to do it up a bit, too."

Our minds fastened onto his idea with youthful tenacity. The obvious thing was simply to take possession and move camp beds in at the first opportunity. But a more honest and more attractive course was to find the owner and ask permission to use the place for our outings. My father arranged this and within a few days we were given the owner's blessing.

After that we spent several nights at Mid Lairgs. Only the kitchen was ever used. The great range, fuelled with dead pine from a nearby forest, gave all the heat we needed. In the centre of the wide chimney an iron hook dangled from a thick chain, and upon it hung our kettle. At each side of the stove a flattened iron bar was embedded in the wall, and on their ends we had balanced two candles. The latters' insignificant flames were entirely neutralised by the blazing firelight but the atmosphere would not have been complete without them.

Opposite the stove, and forming the rear of the room, was a wooden partition upon which we had fixed an enormous map of the district. The stone slab floor was strewn with coconut mats. Our furniture was both varied and primitive: Jimmy, the practical one, had brought his camp bed; Kenneth chose to sleep in the feeding trough which he had lined with blankets. I spent my nights in a sleeping bag on top of a wooden table which we had found in another room.

The nights at Mid Lairgs were always filled with the products of imagination. As the light faded from the vacant moor a musty chill settled in the room despite the fire's heat; we began to feel that we were intruding on the age-long silence and emptiness of the place, yet the nights were never entirely free from sound. When the fire's crackling had died down and we were settled in our makeshift beds I used to listen to the voice of age.

At the very end of that year came the climax to our visits to the farmhouse. It was New Year's Eve, and our intention was to climb Beinn a Bheurlaich and see the old year out from its summit. We had arrived at the farm in the late afternoon when the dusk was beginning to fall over a world white with snow. Of the old trio only Jimmy and I were left; Kenneth had gone to the war. Norman, however, made up the threesome and his unquenchable enthusiasm and boisterous good humour did much to make the excursion a success.

As soon as we had made the fire, Norman and I set out for the hill with a view to finding a reasonable route for the dark journey at midnight. Jimmy volunteered to stay behind, and cook. We climbed the hill in little less than an hour; the snow reflected what light there was in the sky and up until seven o'clock—when we returned to the farm—there was little to prevent one from keeping up a smart pace.

The kitchen was a cheerful place after the cold, dark moor outside. Jimmy had built a sweltering fire and set out candles all round the room. A piping hot meal of bacon and sausages was awaiting our attention and even the beds had been made up; about the latter, experience had made us sage. Gone was the horse-trough in its function as a bed; it now did better service as a seat. Our three camp beds were neatly arranged around the fire.

We were a happy trio as we sat around the blaze waiting for the kettle to boil, hanging from its massive chain. We spoke of the things most young men speak about and recalled many an experience together. Outside the sky had rapidly thickened and within an hour heavy snow was beginning to fall. This did not deter us. We had expected adverse weather and we were ready for it.

It was our intention to reserve an hour and a half for the ascent of the hill in darkness. We all carried torches and both Jimmy and I were very familiar with the ground. If all went according to our schedule we should be at the top of Beinn a Bheurlaich by a quarter to twelve, and back at the farm by a quarter past one on the following morning.

Conversation had begun to fail long before the time set for our departure. The warmth of the fire and the drowsy snow sound outside combined to dissuade us from any further activity and we had difficulty in keeping ourselves awake. In fact I had nodded off briefly when I heard Jimmy say:

"Time to go!"

We pulled warm sweaters over our tousled heads and complained bitterly at this self-imposed punishment. Then we loaded the fire with logs, refilled the kettle and walked out into the night.

Between the blustery showers it was not entirely dark. The stars shone with brilliant lustre and the moorland's great cloak of snow drew and reflected their light. As we joined the heather track below the bridge a shooting-star, released from the apex of the blue-black dome above us, swept down the sky and vanished behind the summit stones of Beinn na Cailleach on the other side of the pass. But to the east the horizon was thick with coming storm and within a few minutes of our leaving the farm the long fingers of a ragged cloud began to wrap themselves round the high slopes of the moorland.

From the bridge I glanced back at the building, a black shape against the snowy background. But for a few sparks coming from the chimney and the faint glow of a candle left in the window it looked as forlorn as when we had first found it.

As a bluster of snow quenched the stars it became totally dark; without our torches we could not have moved an inch. Overawed by this fact we walked in almost unbroken silence and only spoke when it seemed necessary to adjust our course; yet in each heart a little nucleus of the adventure spirit remained alive. Here we were, three glimmers of consciousness in the wilderness of the night, slowly advancing into invisible territory at a time when even the owl had closed its bright eyes in sleep. No sound save the long whine of the wind and the soft crunch of our footfalls reached our ears, we felt little beyond the icy lash of hail upon our cheeks.

The track, so familiar by day, was a tortuous thing of mystery by night, with unknown ramifications and uncertain turns that led we knew not where. For over a mile some sixth sense led us on. Then the inevitable happened. We missed our way and struggled in squelching bog and deep heather. We assumed that we had dropped below the path and accordingly set a course straight up the hillside by feeling, rather than seeing, the slope. But soon we were losing height again having crossed some hummock and we were close to despair when, quite by chance, a familiar boulder was caught in the tiny light-cone of our torches. Then we rested. We were still well on time for we knew that the summit was no more than a mile distant.

Now we were guided by the remnants of an old fence. We had not travelled more than two hundred yards along it when each of us became aware of something quite unusual—but, because it *was* so odd, none of us mentioned it at once. I felt that I had to make sure that what I saw surrounding my two friends' heads was simply the result of straining my eyes in the gloom. I closed my eyes tightly but when I opened them nothing had changed. In fact the manifestation had spread to the tops of their shoulders.

By now I was thoroughly alarmed. My friends' silence was more disturbing than the thing itself. It could not possibly have escaped their notice—that is, if it existed outside of my own mind. I felt compelled to speak.

"Look," I said, "there's something going on. Don't either of you chaps..."

"Well I do," said Norman, "I don't know about Jimmy. But I reckon we've all sprouted halos. At first I thought I was imagining it. Nice to know I'm not!"

"Torches out, then!"

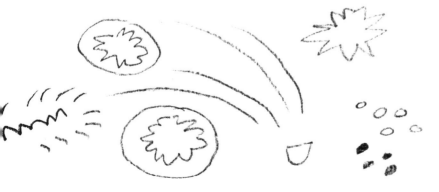

In the black night three faint circles of blue light emanated from brighter centres on the crowns of our heads. We held up our hands with fingers spread and each finger-tip produced a tiny glow. I thought that I experienced a sense of pins and needles but neither Jimmy nor Norman felt anything. It was the former who said, minutes later, "Look at the fence!" And indeed each iron post still upright was busily making its little stream of blue fire. The wind had dropped and in the comparitive silence we could hear a gentle hissing. I have been told that this was St. Elmo's Fire, but nobody has really explained it to me. We talked about it excitedly, almost forgetting the time. Then, helped by a few stars that had emerged behind the snow squall, we made a dash for the top. It wanted five minutes to midnight when we left the fence and scrambled up a well-known rock directly beneath the cairn.

Suddenly the night became deathly calm. It was as though the storms were still and quiet in homage to the dying year. There was a sense of suspense in the passing of the last minutes. We sat around the cairn in the drifted snow, each silent and busy with his own thoughts. I do not know what considerations grave or gay were in my friends' minds, what resolutions made or what thanks were given. To me it was a rare moment, quietly symbolical. I wondered indeed, if I were not a little selfish in making so much of my moment here, amid the hills where I was happy, when on the battlefields of the world—and in the cities torn by the war-flame—men and women were praying for a surcease of sorrow.

So I prayed for peace as midnight stole across the mountains and issued in the bloody year of 1941. Now every star in the firmament was ablaze and, being but young, I think we took it as a sign peace was close.

It was too cold to linger at the cairn and we came down from the hill at a spanking pace. Back at the farm we welcomed the warm kitchen and the sight of our beds drawn up around the fire. We sat down on the inverted trough and pulled off our surplus sweaters. The water was simmering in the old kettle and Jimmy flung a handful of tea into it. Then he produced three fat cheese rolls and offered them round. We munched tiredly in silence but over enormous mugs of tea the conversation started up anew. The talk was mainly concerned with the phenomenal display on the hill, but the tea and the warmth made us reminiscent and we scraped the pot of memory to the dregs.

Once in bed I tossed and turned but could not sleep. My excited mood became subdued and nostalgic. Depression was not far away. I thought of the six wonderful years in which mountains and climbing them had always been close to my mind, and of how the friends with whom I shared them would soon be cast far and wide by the chances of war. Perhaps, after it was all over, we should never be reunited. I hated the war because I knew that, soon or late, somehow or other, it was going to curtail my freedom.

Eventually I drifted towards sleep. Another squall was rattling the house causing the firelight to leap and fall. My last waking thought was of the time, often remembered, when I—a child from the flat lands of East Anglia—had first trod, alone, a little hill...

The First Soft Notes

It was years ago, and the object of my growing infatuation was a little crag amply clad in moss and heather, and glorious then with flaming broom. Overhead there was was a full blue sky for it was a midsummer noon, and in the air was the drone of bees, the cuckoo's voice and the heavy, delicious aroma of the pines.

Then I saw the world through the eyes of a child. I felt it with the untried emotions of those protected years—bright, and filled with promise. It was at this essentially receptive stage in my growth that I climbed my first hill.

How difficult it is to gauge accurately the depth and extent of an impression when time has passed! In trying to recall these thoughts it is hard not to utilise what one has read in order to eke out one's own descriptive powers. Ruskin must not have had a hand in the painting of my clouds, nor Wordsworth in the quietness of my evenings. Nor must I exceed sobriety in my recollections, for mental reactions to natural beauty are not subject to accurate scrutiny and can be easily embroidered. There is a limit to what I have seen: but none to what I have felt.

I was a young boy, then: and very happy to be in the sun. The hills were wonderful things, seen even from a distance. Now I was approaching one. A gate let me into a glade cut deeply in a youthful forest of pine; this glade narrowed to a path, a narrow corridor walled in by clustered pine-trees and carpeted by moss. The path went over undulating ground for a few hundred yards and then climbed steeply up a crag. You may understand the eager anticipation with which I approached the ascent.

Everything was new to me here. As I moved upwards I became aware of a tri-dimensional world; my earlier life's impression had been of a two-dimensional extent of fields and hedgerows with now and then a haystack to suggest a third. Visibility here had evaded the limitations placed upon it by curvature. There was a large and remote horizon with mountains, and a great stretch of sea that bent its nether limits to the sky. At my every step the outlook broadened and became richer in wonders.

My path led through a deep leafy tunnel which was filled with pine scents and the piercing sweetness of the broom. Now and then the sun shone through a gap in the leaves and cast a cloud of gold upon the forest floor. Quite suddenly I reached a place where the trees were withdrawn from the path and to my left rose a steep wall of rock. This was an arrogant place, filled with forbidding crevices in which gorse bushes grew. It was the first time, if my memory does not play me false, that I had seen a naked rock of such a size: and the sight filled me with a curious joy. I was overcome with a primitive desire to climb over its provocative outline. Only the fact that this way did not seem to lead to the summit of the hill deterred me.

There was another world of joyful mystery on the other side of the crag that I was yet to see. Thus far the closely planted pine-trees had excluded much of the view. Soon the path reached a stretch of bare hillside, an escarpment up which it crept by means of crevices and cracks. The incline was still very easy and the surface far from smooth, but thus compelled to climb I learned that there was more in the use of hands and balance than I had realised in my ignorance. My movements were clumsy and hastily executed; my body opposed to my desires; my feet were disinclined to remain where I placed them. Moreover, a slight panic was beginning to overcome me while I was still only half-way up. Dry-mouthed, I contemplated a retreat.

A glance downwards soon convinced me that this course of action would be ill-advised, for the rock beneath me appeared yet more formidable than from above. I began to rail at myself for having attempted something that so obviously exceeded my powers (and heartily wished that I might stand once again upon the horizontal earth). Ten minutes of this indecision passed and the need for self-discipline grew apparent. At the most I would only receive a shaking, I concluded; and, having studied the remainder of the slope and seen numerous possibilities, I dismissed the panic and climbed quickly to the summit. Here all difficulty was ended and the path continued at an easier angle towards the crest of the hill.

The sharp rise had carried me clear of the encircling trees and a wonderful world lay at my feet. There were houses, fields and hedges: there was a river between hills, and a road that climbed the crinkled hills like a piece of discarded lace. Lit by the bright sun, this world was painted in the most vivid colours and lay in absolute peace. Noise is utterly foreign to the hills when the winds and rains are absent. That long blue water yonder might have borne the fabled halcyon on its calm surface.

Then came the wind and went by me with a cry. To me it was a new kind of wind; there was something deep and robust in it, wonderfully free and undomesticated. In it were to be found the elements, stories of sea coves and swelling tides. This was no town wind, bitter with the pollutions of a ravaged countryside; this breeze had tasted snow and heather and rocks drenched in the upland dew. In it was the very spirit of the mountains.

Raising my face to the sky I breathed deep draughts of air. Having renewed my strength, I continued to climb. For some distance the path was again concealed in a sheath of pine trees and I could see nothing beyond my immediate surroundings.

But soon I knew that the crest of the hill was not far away. Everything suggested its proximity. The slope rose for a final flourish of ascent and I quickened my pace to a run and covered the last hundred yards in a few minutes. There I stood, wrapt in the wind and the golden sun, with the unseen aura of my expanding spirit above my head—and not a sound escaped me, for the tremendous turmoil of my mind prevented all activity beyond it.

As I sit here now, straining the chords of memory in an attempt to portray accurately my far-off reaction, I can but faintly visualise the scene although it is one that I now know well: but I can still feel the spirit in me springing into renewed life.

There was water, and sky, and mountains—near and far, small and great; there were trees that caught the fiery promise of the sunset in their waving branches. There was my friend, the wind, coming up the hillside with the soft music of its sigh. The miracle of distance gripped my thoughts into a focal point and welded my desires to the bars of resolution. Above all, those mountains, what were they? These single things—water, rock, soil, air and fire—had been brought as one in my mind to form a coherent whole.

These then were my impressions. Much has been lost in the passage of years—colour, detail and mood. Yet the desire to recapture and express has compelled me, time and again, like an unskilled artist to set them to canvas in chaotic daubs and curious splashes, bringing their sincerity to discredit and murdering the thought with my rough treatment.

Sobering thought came of later years. If there was philosophy in the mind of that mortal on the little hill it was the inconsistent one of youth, as unstable as the wind from which it came. My eyes were filled with sunset and blue water. I keenly anticipated the day when I would penetrate the distances and see those far grey mountains close at hand. There was little intellectual pleasure.

Some time had passed and the sunset glow had deepened. I made to depart but so great was the spell that a force outside myself restrained me until dusk followed closely upon the heels of the sunset and the wind fell. A great calm filled the summer's evening.

Then I walked down into the teeming darkness of the pine wood. There was a whispering in the grass, a bird hopped across the path and regarded me with interest: he showed no fear of me and it was only when a great flapping indicated the flight of a wood-pigeon through the trees that he made off. Watching a squirrel spring up a slab of rock I marvelled at the lissom ease with which the creature moved. There and then I longed to be lithe and strong, to feel the demand for movement in my muscles and the call of adventure in my heart.

I walked down the hill with my head held high and drank in the beauty of the night. Above me the sky was a cavern of royal blue inset with gems of light. The footpath strewn with the leaves was soft to my feet. In my heart's depths there lingered the provocative mystery of the mountains, their distant beauty and compelling appeal. As I saw it then—an integral part in the great mystery of human existence—I see and feel it now. My mind has crept through the tortuous channels of thought to the age-old question "What is beyond? What is before? Is there a plan?" For those who have formed a deep and intimate relationship with the wild and mountainous places of the earth there is still no answer, but there is an intuitive belief that the question itself is of less import than some would believe. To me there is much value in the simple perception and appreciation of beauty.

The sun is high in the heavens and the seasons go their ways and for my part, I do not doubt that we too, without effort or the taking of thought, shall come back with the upturning of our chance. But if not, and the bright vapour of our soul is dissipated in the long void of unending night, then there is still less need for our frantic prostrations before the altars of the shadowy, created gods of the present days.

Thus, twelve years earlier, in the manner described, the love of the mountains and the beginnings of their strength had entered into my heart.

The Way of the Eagle

*F*ar above us he soared and his golden wings were like kindred stars in the deep blue of the sky: we, for our parts, strove to find a means of support on the great grey rock face beneath him.

My friend had seen him first. He had been delicately negotiating a shallow crack in the face of the slab while my attention was turned to securing him from beneath. He had been giving a continuous commentary upon the climb when suddenly he fell silent. I looked up. His eyes were also turned upwards and I followed their direction.

The crag we were climbing was not unusually spectacular in the dramatic fashion of better-known hills. There were no pinnacles, deep gullies, no buttresses and no narrow ridges. There was simply a long hillside, very steep but mostly heather-clad and boulder-strewn, and in the middle there was a small stream: our crag was to the left. If one looked along the hillside it could be seen that the general angle was exceeded a few degrees by the line of the crag, just sufficient to preclude heather from growing on the granite face except where ledges existed, which in some places almost girdled the crag, and were thick with vegetation, giving rise to a strange effect: if one was climbing (and looking) upwards, the rock face seemed to be of unbroken granite, but if one looked downwards only the ledges were conspicuous and gave the impression of merely a steep hillside.

THE WAY OF THE EAGLE

The sun was hot upon our backs as we climbed for there was a cloudless sky and hardly a breath of wind. We had come across a curious, scree-filled gully which slanted upwards across the precipice. What had looked like a continuous granite face beyond it now turned out merely to be a succession of smooth slabs separated by wide ledges. The most disappointing thing about this was that at any point one could simply wander away on to the hillside by means of one of these terraces. In my youthful fervour the term "No other way!" was an exciting one: but here if the going became stiff you could just walk off the precipice. I did not like this arrangement.

From where I sat the crag arched like a dome above. Suddenly the blue sky was rent by a wand of gold. Great wings outspread, proud head levelled with his flight, the bird sailed over us.

Though aware of our presence, he showed neither anger nor fear. Twice, three times, he circled the rock, and each time he had risen in the sky. He disappeared for a time and then came again, this time far above us. Finally he saw something in the depths of the glen, something our eyes could not decipher amid rocks, bog and heather, and he shot through the blue air in a long, swift descent. He passed through the afternoon that lingered on the heights into the evening beginning in the glen.

He was my first eagle. And this was my first real climb. With the fervent enthusiasm—amounting almost to fanaticism—that characterises a sensitive child, I had embraced the mountains as my natural god. There was little of the idealist in me but much of the acrobat. With my friends, I had swarmed over every modest crag that parental jurisdiction had permitted: much more we would have done, if this restraining factor had been absent, but I cannot think that we would have survived. We had some miraculous escapes and did many remarkable things.

The man who was with me on this occasion was a mature mountaineer. He based his pleasure, very properly, on the margin of safety that a climb gave him; the thoughtless use of the scales in which life and death are hung was not for him. He loved the mountains more than the rocks, the freedom more than the excitement, the beauty more than the fear. No better mentor could I have had on my first real venture.

The crag on which we were climbing had the Gaelic name, Creag Liath, 'the grey cliff'—a happy and descriptive title. Beneath our feet the valley wound away and through it the river meandered like the body of a big snake. Mountains stood up on every side, rising in a blue haze. Beinn na Caoraich, 'the Sheep's Hill', opposite us across the glen, rose in bulky, shapely flanks of heather and stone; Beinn Ruadh, 'the Red Hill' looked over its shoulder; other mountains standing by the sea flung up their spires like remote mystical cathedrals.

Towards evening a great calm descended upon the mountains. The distant streams seemed to fall in slower measure; there was conspiracy in the blue caverns of the sky. High as we were, there was little wind to disperse the heat; beneath the final precipice we flung ourselves down on a ledge of heather.

It had been an exciting and memorable day for me. My friend had expressed a favourable opinion of my climbing; the few words he said served to raise me to the seventh heaven of delight! Then he turned his attention to the next—and last—part of the climb. He did not seem pleased by what he saw and even to my unpractised eye it was apparent that here the climbing was of a different order to that which we had already experienced. The crag, as already mentioned, was formed by a bulge of the hillside, which for the greater part of its height rose parallel to it. But near the top it took on a higher angle and drew away from the slope in a kind of final flourish. On this terminal section grass and heather refused to grow and a gray slab reared up in a formidable manner.

After examination of the problem my friend pointed out a narrow fracture that seemed to cleave the slab in a vertical direction. He instructed me carefully what to do in the event of a mishap, saw that I was securely bound to a prominent rock and climbed slowly into the foot of the groove.

31

For twenty feet his progress was steady. For another five yards short
upward movements alternated with moments of apparent reflection.
Then it seemed that the reflections became gloomy, for all movement
ceased.

"I don't like this!" I heard him say.

I must admit that at this moment I was indulging in one of those flights
of fancy familiar to my age, in which my friend was condemned to come to

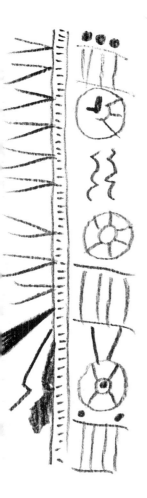

grief in the next few minutes and I was to save him from a fatal fall. With the thought of this dramatic possibility I was tying the rope in knots about me and waiting—to my shame, let it be said!—almost in impatience for the mishap which would straight-way convert me into a hero. But it did not come. Very carefully he retraced his steps and presently stood beside me on the ledge. There was a trace of amusement in his eyes as he glanced at the abominable tangle which my zeal had made of the rope.

"You were making sure I see! That's a hard section ahead. I advise you to take care on it."

"Me?" I gasped, hardly believing my ears.

"Yes. Why not? I don't like the look of it, but there isn't any risk. I'm heavier and stronger than you are and can easily hold you if you come off. In any case, you would only slide down the slab. You'll find a small overhang near the top. Its mainly a question of balance, but once over that you'll be up."

A tremendous elation filled me at the thought of leading a climb which he had adjudged to be difficult. Scarcely waiting for him to secure himself I approached the base of the crack and cautiously entered it. Easy climbing led to where the crack faded out in a smooth slab. About fifteen feet above me a wall of rock stood out from the slab, obviously the barrier that had troubled my friend. I accomplished the intervening distance; now the wall, no more than five feet in height, seemed an insuperable barrier. Each time I tried to rise to my feet I was aware of its pressure against my shoulder. Time and again I tried to work myself into a position where I could reach out for some handholds high above my head. At last, bybending to the side as well as backwards I found a deep incut groove for my fingers of the left hand. For my right I could find nothing. This did not alarm me at first but soon my legs began to ache and I wondered if the

33

movement was reversible. I sensed that it was not as soon as I thought about it and a sudden wave of dread engulfed me.

My fingers were beginning to tire and tiny piercing sensations ran down my arm where it was pressed awkwardly against the bulge. I glanced down at my friend: he was seated in a secure position and was by no means unaware of my physical discomfort and mental agony. In view of his attention I assumed an appearance of nonchalance, but I was far from feeling it.

"It isn't easy" I admitted, " but I'll rest for a moment and then try again. I can't find another handhold over the bulge." He said nothing but readjusted his strong position to one of even greater security. The sight gave me some encouragement and I made another attempt to find a niche. This time luck favoured me. A tiny rib of quartz stood out of the smoothness of the slab and my fingers closed over it gratefully. Without considering whether worse might be to come I drew myself up quickly, found a foothold and swung over the bulge.

"Very good!" my friend said. There was no further climbing to be done; I seated myself in a firm position and waited for him to join me. Together we scrambled up the steep heather and broken rock until we reached the summit of Creag Liath.

The evening had climbed up the long slopes and was now upon us here. It was as if all the beauty in the world had been drawn into the measure of these few miles and into this brief moment. Nothing but the memory can make such a prospect permanent, and it seems to me now that much of this was a projection of my own transitory joy.

The sun was hanging over the western sea. Beneath it the level surface had turned to a line of molten gold, an attenuated bubble of light that seethed and foamed in blue water and bluer hills. The crags behind us had undergone a subtle change in colour, they had lost the material solidness of the day: almost transparent, in places one could sense the pale sky behind, while the more distant hills were merely lines without depth, only fore-knowledge of their presence distinguishing them from clouds.

The river which ran far beneath us was serpentine, a curling, twisting thing that had set its own course in a moment of lunacy long ago. A river of evening, slow and very peaceful. The valley at our feet was long and level, fashioned by glaciers in ancient days, and on its floor and the slopes to the east, the shadowed mountains were staggered in weird outlines. The crag fell away in a succession of giant heather-clad steps beneath us. Now a little wind blew out of the glen and brought with it the scents of the summer maturity. The recollection of smell is never held tenaciously by the mind, and it is curious to observe in contrast how brilliantly and with what poignancy scents can recover mental associations.

When we had rested and admired the scene for nearly an hour we started to descend into the glen by the steep slope adjacent to the crag. At the bottom, on a strip of grassy land was a tumbledown cottage in which we had left a little food. We sat between the four walls on a wooden floor and enjoyed some sandwiches and a flask of coffee as we spoke about our climb. From the few words we said an observant witness could discover the diversity of our approach to the mountains. To my friend, a devotee of many years standing, they represented the best single part of life in which all other parts were mixed in some proportion. To me, a comparitive newcomer, they were the source of a fanatical and uncomplicated enthusiasm. My companion found that thoughts of the high places made the dull round of daily, ordinary life more tolerable; to me the least suggestion of a mountain served to arouse a revolt against ordinary things. My mind was eager, extravagant and prodigal, jealous of time spent in other places, always yearning for the crags. Mine was then the eagle's way, the way of the empty, joyous spaces and the long fields of air.

The day was drawing to a close but the atmosphere was as calm and warm as if it had still been noon. With half-closed eyes, knowing that it was time for us to go but each waiting for the other to make the first move in the homeward direction, we might have drifted into sleep had not a bright star suddenly flashed across my vision, a tiny speck far above the bastions which were still faintly sun-flushed. It was the eagle. He soared and dropped and soared again while we, shamed from our somnolent states by the show of energy, prepared to take the track out of the glen. We turned for a final glance and as we did so we saw him plunge through the evening of the crag-tops into the ascending darkness of the glen to strike savagely at his prey.

The Dwelling-place of Beauty

A grouse flew up and hurried away across the moor with a soft beating of wings and a great chattering, while the big shadow of a cloud spread across the long undulation of the hillside.

Otherwise all was silently drowsy. The moors, lightly veiled by a thin mist, lay glimmering beneath the pale winter's sunshine which even now was beginning to weaken as the rays lengthened and the source of their origin slanted down towards the distant hills. Beasts, birds, were hidden in their holes or secreted in the lower valleys. All of the animal world was asleep, but the grouse, actuated by an inner impulse, flew on.

Over the heathery uplands it flew, and above deep declivities in whose depths ran streams. It is in such places that the large rivers, springing deeply from hidden subterranean vaults, have their origins. Across breasts of fern and moss it sped. And, at last, after it had begun to seem as if this journey were prompted by mere joie-de-vivre rather than the pursuance of a definite object, it singled out a particular stone and alighted upon it.

Beneath the bird's rock a deep stream had, by a myriad years of unceasing motion, worn itself a gorge. The stream tumbled over stones, continually twisting in its course as it went; here it would spring and rush down a marble channel into an emerald pool fringed with shadows; there it would run with a slow, stately and measured pace through long marshes. Surrounded by lines of black peat, the waters ran as though it were a struggle to continue. When suddenly, the waters burst, with a loud and hollow roar, into a confined and steeply sloping passage. Even higher there hung a wooden bridge.

From the path that ran near the bottom of the ravine I had climbed the slope. The complete absence of life made me feel a little uncomfortable and had some aquatic being appeared I should have been more comforted than bewildered. The bridge was so constructed that only two beams of doubtful strength and a knotted cord stood between me and a drop of disconcerting depth: but the scene quite compensated for the insecurity of the position. The thin hiss of the waters in the cascade, their deeper rumble in the upper reaches blended to form a strange and primitive music.

I crossed the bridge, seated myself on the twisted roots of an ancient tree and gave up my mind to that peculiar state of mental perception in which the smallest impulse from without creates a world of thought within. I half-closed my eyes and listened, intent upon detecting any sound distinct from that of the cataract.

The air was so cool, so poignant with the scent of frosted heather, while the sun sparkled; yet there was a sense of unhappiness, a deep ache at the core of the heart, with a feeling of something unrevealed—an intuition so potent that it brought my spread thoughts back to their fountain-head. Then it came to me with strength and decision, an involuntary suggestion, that in this scene was the nucleus of Reality, bitterly beautiful.

The mountains faced me calm and impassive. The ice would come, the ice would melt away; the trees would lose their leaves, and put on their verdure once again. The rabbits would jump: and presently their lungs would inhale no more. What was once blood and flesh would become a mould that sinks into the mountain turf. In its place, would come another animal.

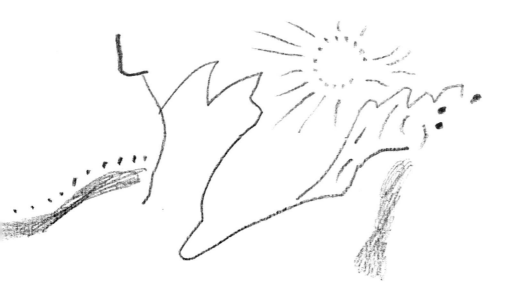

I found comfort in the terrible thought that if I were to die then and there my remains would be translated, through an infinity of time and space, through firmaments and atoms, back to this shape, this moment and this thought.

For a few moments I became unaware of my own identity, as though the spirits of the thousand men and creatures who had looked upon the cascade from most distant times had entered my body and were gazing through my eyes. I was possessed by the spirit of the ages and felt in a swift, all-embracing impulse, the wild surmise of primitive intuition; and my soaring spirit fell as, returning to myself, I found that these ages had taught *me* nothing.

Near the pine-root on which I had been seated a small path led away into the valley. Here the hills closed in to contain a narrow ravine; at its entrance stood a building. The idea of a habitation in this lonely place appealed to me; the prospect of exchanging a few words with a fellow mortal after a day of loneliness was a good one.

I strode away down the path. The sun was very low in the western sky: its pale beams struck the summits of the higher hills, but in the valley the darkness fell like dew. A dark mist rose over the river. Distantly a fox barked; a bird cried shrilly. I shivered. My comfort and ecstasy were gone.

I was a quarter of a mile from the building when I saw it was deserted. I hesitated to approach for doubts clouded my mind and I was afraid of shadows. But I disciplined myself to continue; I approached slowly, glancing from right to left.

The front door, encircled by twisted hawthorn, hung on its hinges. I pushed it open and gazed inside. When my eyes had become accustomed to the gloom I saw two rooms divided by a broken partition, a crumbling fireplace, and a floor strewn with discoloured plaster.

There was rank age in the house, a deep atmosphere of rot. It seemed older than the mountains upon whose roots it rested. I listened intently. The old rooms were filled with sound. Something whispered, there was a dripping of water, and a rustling that I could not explain. Then a door closed; at this I made to run outside but restrained myself. These fears were baseless and cowardly creations; I was afraid of a shadow born of shadows. An insidious light began to pervade the room: a great moon bathed in a sea of blood rose through the mists of the river and shone upon the frost-girdled valley. I greeted this goddess; gradually the world became a place of magic, of mysterious glades and a strip of translucent river. Opposite me there was a steep hillside where sheep showed as white, vague shapes. It was so beautiful that I lost all my former fears; before me was presented something of infinite power. What was this atmosphere? I cannot tell. But there was a deep music in the mist; not the rush of the river—a softer and more mellow note. It rose and fell as the moonbeams flickered; it died away in the infinity of the distant stars. I did not think that this music was engendered in my mind; it seemed to come from the womb of the earth itself, creeping up through seams in the soil and rock.

There is harmony between Nature and the mind that loves her. The thoughts that arose from the utterly grand scene were in harmony; but they were too *simple* for my brain, fed on vanity, to comprehend. This was the pivot upon which all my mental life, my highest aspirations revolved. This was the power that made music and poetry and art, this elemental sympathy. I looked up at the sky and followed the silver tracks of the stars. I drew in the vast intuition of infinite distance. I longed to be free of the body that limited my whereabouts; the ego that limited my scope. I longed to break the steel hoops of emotionalism that bound me to the human world. My mind struggled to rise above outworn creeds and the tired social aspirations that drive men to deeds of incredible futility.

Somewhere in the house a door banged again, and a small animal scuttled across the floor. The wind rose and began to roar and roll in the hollow roof and to agitate a broken window frame. All at once I was enthused with a desire for action; there was a cool nip in the air which was a physical stimulant. Leaving the house for the steep slope of the hill opposite, I felt the blood throb as the muscles of my legs anticipated the upward climb. It was as though the cold rays of the moon had flung their icy energy into the channels of my body. Higher and higher my bounding steps carried me until great pits of peat, crested with bristling heather, were all around me: here and there a white stone flashed in its dusky setting.

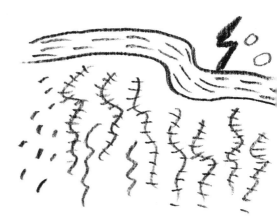

As the slope increased my energy mounted as I sprang over boulders, through thudding corridors of peat, and across tiny streams. The hollow wind, romping round the moorland lent me the wildness of its race for a season and the winds that hurry through the void and empty air became mine. There was nothing now to arrest my physical caprice, no part of this moonlit world was barred for it had become light and thin and spun away beneath my feet. I now hung motionless in time as, springing up upon my pulsing brain, my soul reached the highest fields of ecstasy as it embraced the sum of all created things. Reaching up into the sky, I could drag down the stars to resolve them into glittering dew upon the mountain grass.

Gradually, the slope began to fail as the mountain gathered itself up into its final folds, and my soul no longer could contain the expanding Psyche: it broke out of the prison of the skull and, as from a great height I seemed to see the tiny figure fall on its knees in an act of pagan worship upon a hilltop.

What is this soul, so great that it can create and fashion a world, so small that it can be confined within a bony cage? What are these mountain acres, the silvery river, the hovering moon—so huge and clear that one wonders why it is so silent—or the cold stone under feet? Psyche replies with the intuition of rapture that there is one prospect for them all, and that is *of return*.

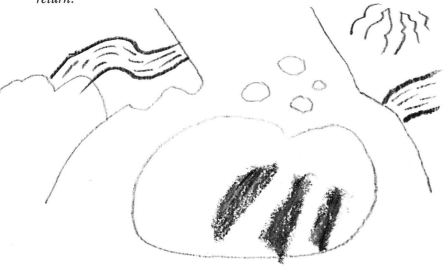

I have been here before, a whisper tells me, but Psyche insists—you are always here, there is no beginning and no end for everything returns. If you are happy now you will always be happy, but if sad you cannot escape that sadness. Let the long ages pass, let the earth go and come again, you

will be translated back, through bursting suns and aching cold, through all the weird and savage living shapes, to this hillside in this same night!

I rose and walked slowly round the summit. There was a deep, bitter cold on the night wind that told me that it was very late: it was time that I was going. No longer was I the unfettered child of a durable Nature, but the inhabitant of a mutable world to which I was bound by the chains of custom. Psyche returned inside my skull, the ecstatic drug had worn off and left my mind—and indeed my body—limp and tired.

On my way down I found two solitary trees whose branches were tangled in a long embrace, their arms seeming to implore the heavens to strike them asunder from an eternal posture. Soon my path led me once again beside the long-sounding river, where frost had begun to load the trees with its glittering burden: night pressed down upon the mountains, and upon my spirit. My path climbed over a shoulder of the hill, and at the top I was startled to see a vague shape huddled in the deep heather and to hear the complaint of a tiny voice. It was a little lamb, couched by his mother, and while he regarded me with neither curiosity nor fear his eyes seemed fixed upon distant things, far beyond me or my kind, and they were filled with infinite wisdom.

tHe VaLhalla OF ROCKS

After three years' apprenticeship to the mountains I was adjudged an efficient enough climber to perform in the Island of Skye under the care of an experienced friend. Ever since my interest had become centred on hills Skye had been an obsession with me. We arrived at the Sligachan Hotel in the late evening and a pall of cloud deprived me of my first view of the mountains.

Inside the hotel the photographs of the Cuillin ridge and the records contained in the climbers' books were a consolation for the dark clouds that hid the view. I was incredibly happy to be on the island which had furnished material for a thousand dreams; it was not only the Cuillin that had taken such a strong hold on my imagination: the very thought of "island", such an island, circled by the sun-gilded waters of the Minch, bare in the North, tree-clad in the South, absorbed my whole attention. And now—I was there! My one fear was that the inauspicious weather signs indicated a period of prolonged mist and rain. I stopped reading from time to time and went outside to look at the weather. My friend, who had been visiting Skye and its mountains at regular intervals for many years, assured me that all the signs promised a fine day for the morrow.

It was quite late when I laid aside the pages of the Climbers' Book and went to bed, and my last action (as one might expect) was to glance out of my window at a great pall of moonlit cloud that hung over the mountain that I longed to see. It was early when I woke, but the sun was streaming in through chinks in the curtain. For a moment I lay still, trying to recollect my whereabouts in the unfamiliar room. In the back of my mind there was a growing belief that something very important and very pleasant was pending discovery and then, in the middle of both a stretch and yawn, remembered what information was knocking on my mental door.

Skye! To be here, in Skye—at the very feet of these wonderful mountains—with the bright morning sunshine outside! Sgurr nan Gillean, that rose at the head of the moorland: the mental image of the scene was very familiar to me from pictures: in my mind, now, I followed the crest over the pinnacle ridge, Am Basteir, the tooth, Sgurr a Bhasteir—all the well-imagined peaks!

The sun was shining in at the window. I did not doubt the hills would be clear of mist as I sprang out of bed and a few steps carried me to the window.

My hands reached up to draw the curtains aside. I hesitated, suddenly afraid of an anti-climax or, more likely, anxious to savour the moment to the full. Then, in brilliant colour and faithful to an outline that I already knew by heart, the scene burst upon my eyes like an explosion. My most vivid imaginings had fallen far, far short of the magnificent reality of it. It was both beautiful and terrible. The rounded contours of the moorland,

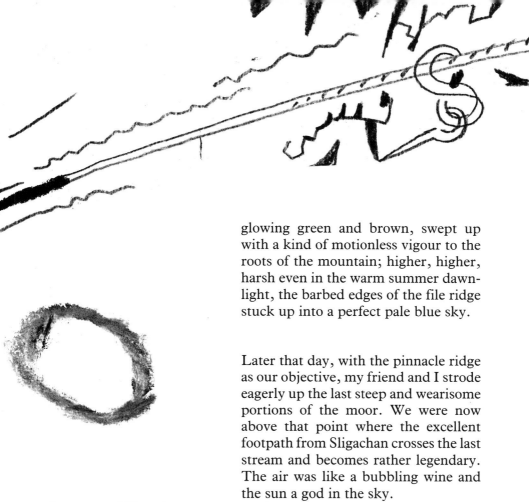

glowing green and brown, swept up with a kind of motionless vigour to the roots of the mountain; higher, higher, harsh even in the warm summer dawn-light, the barbed edges of the file ridge stuck up into a perfect pale blue sky.

Later that day, with the pinnacle ridge as our objective, my friend and I strode eagerly up the last steep and wearisome portions of the moor. We were now above that point where the excellent footpath from Sligachan crosses the last stream and becomes rather legendary. The air was like a bubbling wine and the sun a god in the sky.

Sgurr nan Gillean began to tower above us. I resented the loose stones that made an occasional glance at the ground a necessary precaution. I wanted simply to feast my eyes on the outline of the hill.

Beneath the prominent vertebrae of the Pinnacle Ridge there is an indistinct coccygeal remain, a low ridge which is demarcated on the one hand by the savage Basteir ravine and on the other by the rock-girt cup of Coire Ruadh. Once the beginning of this craggy tail is reached the hardest part of the approach to the mountain is over; from there one walks on air with the stimulating image of the great ridge gaining in size every step one takes. Never have I been so thrilled as I was then with the great rock-walls of Cuillin rising on every side. The squat, brooding bulk of Blaven dominated the end of Glen Sligachan. The scimitar shape of the Basteir Tooth cut the sky westward.

When we reached a point directly beneath the crags of the first pinnacle, we seated ourselves upon a rock and ate our lunch of sandwiches. Although keen appetites made the simple fare delicious my whole attention was riveted upon the rocks which we were about to climb and with eighty feet of Alpine line lay uncoiled at our feet my excitement reached fever pitch!

The crags leading to the summit of the first pinnacle did not prove difficult but gave us invigorating work for hands and feet, and it was not long before my friend and I gained the broken crest of the ridge. I was rather disappointed to find that the pinnacle was not truly deserving of its name; on its south flank it was merely a hundred feet of sloping scree, for the ridge does not really begin before the third pinnacle.

We scrambled over easy rocks to the ill-defined second pinnacle and paused there to view the more interesting ground before us. The third one was an imposing object; its base was broad and massive, but higher up much of its bulk diminished and its crest was formed by a rib of narrow rock; yet despite its intimidating appearance there were few barriers betweeen us and the summit of this pinnacle, and after scrambling up exhilaratingly steep rocks we stood on the narrow crest.

This was a dramatic place. In the last hundred feet the nature of the climbing had undergone a radical alteration. At no time during our traverse of the first and second summits were we compelled to follow any definite route; there were a hundred variations to every way we went. But now the route was confined to certain well-known cracks and crevices; each hand or foot hold was polished by the action of a thousand steel-shod boots.

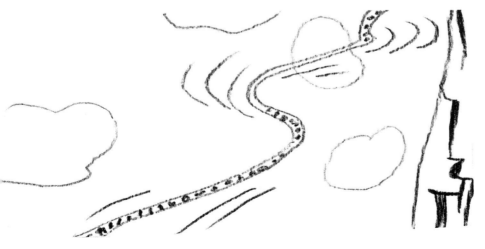

The actual crest of the pinnacle is composed of a few closely jammed boulders which are arched over a stupendous drop. I hung over this grim descent in amazement and gazed into the profound depths of the corrie where some climbers were creeping up a scree-bed nearly a thousand feet beneath us. I was beginning to congratulate myself on getting thus far without difficulty until my friend indicated the next move. It looked most fearsome: a short traverse to the left followed by a descent to a rocky shelf were merely the introductions to a much harder problem—a vertical slab (he assured me it was plentifully blessed with holds) over a tremendous fall.

In view of my obvious trepidation my friend sent me down first. The initial movements were easy. Then I came to the vertical slab. I regarded this in undisguised alarm.

"Down there?" I queried, in order to gain time.

My mentor nodded. "Take it easy though. It's a matter of balance, so keep close in. The holds are good. You're quite safe!"

Few novices have any appreciation of the arresting power of new hemp and I was no exception. To me a slip, rope or no rope, was the end!

Very cautiously then, I backed over the edge of the slab and surveyed the distant corrie through my legs. I cast about for holds but could not find any that appeared adequate. For an experienced mountaineer they were no doubt ample, and indeed the place is not considered severe. For me, little versed in such a problem and balanced precariously over a gruesome plunge, going hot and cold by turns, and beginning to perspire at the finger-tips (which was the last thing I wanted) they seemed insufficient to a degree.

My friend's face indicated that he was finding the situation an amusing one (in view of some brave remarks of mine on an earlier occasion) and I determined to succeed there and then or perish in the attempt! With elaborate care, designed to cover feelings of desperation, I shuffled my feet and tried to reduce the gravitational pull. The key to the whole situation was obviously an ample spike of rock that was embedded in the slab some five feet below me. Cautiously, I felt down the rock face for a low handhold. My fingers closed on a small, firm ledge. I removed one leg from its hold and lowered it towards the vital spike. With my body at full stretch there was still eighteen inches to go; my friend gave me another word of advice, but, without assimilating it, I pulled my other foot away and slithered down to the desired rugosity. This overcame the problem and the expression on my face was not unlike a smirk!

The climbing that followed was less strenuous. We steadily mounted to the summit of the fourth pinnacle, from where Sgurr nan Gillean rose gracefully against the azure sky. Spurred on by the close proximity of our objective we scaled the last steep rocks and in a short time stood upon the small summit of the mountain.

Around us and beneath our feet lay the island. In a semi-circle was the sea, a sky-blue ocean of mid-summer; with wave upon wave of the green mountains of the Scottish mainland behind. The range of Cuillin teeth stuck up behind our backs. Subsequently I made out the graceful incisors of Sgurr Alasdair and the bulky molar formations of Sgurr a Mhadaidh, the wolf's crown.

Just beneath us the ridge twisted and curved away, culminating in the weird outline of Am Basteir: the crag with its bizarre shape comes as a shock to the brain for it is a deformed mountain.

It is a habit of mine, while on a mountain, to close my eyes momentarily in order to to assimilate all the impressions and make room in the mind for more. This I did. I felt the warm sun on my face and smelt the island air, yet when I opened my eyes the whole excessive, lavish glory of the scene smote against my consciousness. Being on a holiday with my friend, free to roam these hills for days, in the full health and strength of youth, I was ecstatically joyful, happier than I had ever been before and, for aught I know, happier than I shall ever be again.

The slow deterioration of the weather that took place during the next few days did nothing to interfere with the vigorous programme we had set ourselves. Rain on the Cuillin, the windy salt-tasting rain blown from the rolling Minch, is an exhilirating element which carries the eternal song of the sea on its breath. It streamed over the rocks we were climbing and ran down our sleeves: it poured into our boots: it attacked every gap in our clothing; it whipped the blood in our faces. But we cared nothing for these discomforts, for the fierce antagonism of the climate did nothing to confound our schemes. Upwards over ridges, loud with the roar of the tempest, we forced our way; and, while feeling with the Stratford Bard that such rough handling was far from flattery, we were confident in our ability to join battle with the hosts of the storm.

On the fifth morning I awoke to hear a subtle change in the voice of the river Sligachan. The usual low rushing note had gone and in its place was a heavily sustained roar that told of much flood-water along its course. Through the window was a scene of waving grass and lashing rain, with Sgurr nan Gillean no more than a misty, phantom mountain, its pinnacles breasting the clouds that sped across it. For this day we had set aside the traverse of Blaven and Clach Glas, the only expedition, as good fortune would have it, that could be undertaken by us in bad weather.

Two hours later however we were debating whether conditions were not so bad as to prevent any expedition at all. The morning hours when the sun should be gaining in strength were unrelievedly dark. At ten o'clock squalls of wind and rain were blowing against the hotel windows in a murky darkness. Half an hour later, however, there was a very slight improvement and my friend decided to motor to the foot of Blaven and wait there for a change.

And so, after some thirty miles we were parked beside Loch Slapin, from where the bulk of Blaven and the narrow ridge of Clach Glas became visible as the clouds fell away from their summits and billowed out into the corries beneath. This was a significant weather sign: we could not however, agree upon its implications. Shortly it stopped raining. We donned our rucksacks and made tracks for the mountain.

Cataracts, overbrimming with the products of twenty hours of rain, coursed down the green slopes of the foothills, foaming past us as we climbed towards the intial ridge. Our four days of climbing had produced a remarkable improvement in our physical condition. Gone was the heavy breathing, the thumping heart-beat and the tired muscle—every step was a joy and the deep, steady respiration added a rhythm to our movements.

Smartly then, we approached the high ridge that bends round to Clach Glas and in a remarkably short time had put most of it behind us.

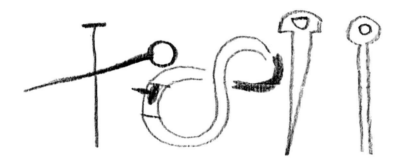

By now we could no longer retain any optimism about the weather. It had grown much darker again and from the upper part of the ridge a Stygian scene met our eyes. To our backs lay a white sea which suggested to me a bloodless skin drawn tightly across unwrinkled flesh: whilst ahead of us were slow-drifting clouds with little fleeces of mist scudding across their paths. The mountains, heavy and prominent, arose out of gloom-filled valleys; forcing themselves upon our notice by reason of the clear, rain-washed atmosphere, their colours funereal and menacing: black and grey struggled with a dusky green for pride of place, and out to sea, a yellowish sickly hue loomed in the sky.

A small wind panted up from the corries. It was a furtive little disturbance, a bastard of the elements which seemed ashamed of its very life. We walked up the grassy ridge without speaking for somehow there was nothing to say: the usual creative want that satisfies itself in conversation was stifled by the heavy menacing atmosphere.

Clach Glas is a very strong, masculine shape, an aggressive rock. We approached it with a degree of apprehension, for it looked a savage place to brave in worsening weather. As we were untying the rope beneath the first rocks a large spot of rain fell on my hand. I looked at my friend, and as deliberate confirmation of our thought a thick tentacle of mist curled around the grey pinnacle above us.

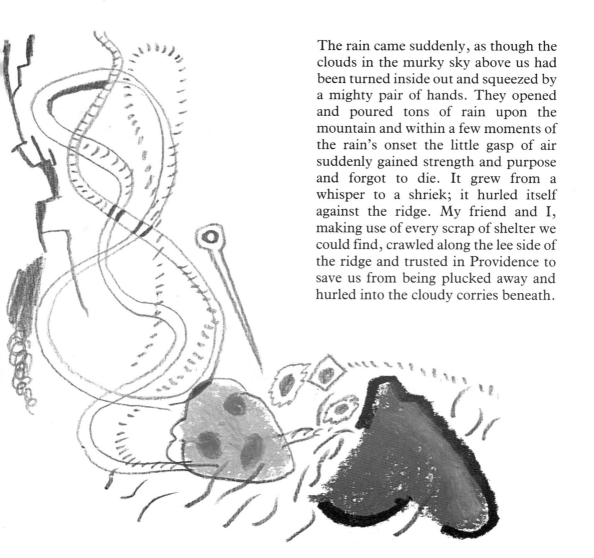

The rain came suddenly, as though the clouds in the murky sky above us had been turned inside out and squeezed by a mighty pair of hands. They opened and poured tons of rain upon the mountain and within a few moments of the rain's onset the little gasp of air suddenly gained strength and purpose and forgot to die. It grew from a whisper to a shriek; it hurled itself against the ridge. My friend and I, making use of every scrap of shelter we could find, crawled along the lee side of the ridge and trusted in Providence to save us from being plucked away and hurled into the cloudy corries beneath.

As the temperature began to fall, the rain turned to a fine sleet. While this was blown on a strong wind it was impossible to proceed, for our eyes watered and closed in the face of it. The cold, however, seemed to seal up the origins of the wind, which soon dropped to a moderate breeze so that we were now able to make much better progress; but constant care had to be exercised in exposed places, due to the deposit of sleet upon the rocks.

Descending the far side of Clach Glas we were presented with a series of tricky corners where a vertical rock-wall barred our path, after which came a long sloping ledge that girdled the great tower of Blaven; around it we crept, and here it was wide and partially sheltered us from the storm; a perilous gap revealed to us a vista of eddying mist and profoundly disturbing turmoil. So heavy was the rain that the water ran down into our clothes and gradually my energies began to wane and I was tired and dispirited when we reached the summit of Blaven.

Under good conditions this is reputed to be a superb viewpoint, but now there was nothing to be seen but a few square yards of short, drenched grass and a sturdy cairn. We waited long enough to pronounce the word "top" and then strode down the opposite side of the hill. Here it became necessary to exercise sound judgement in order to find our correct line of descent. Two hundred yards from the cairn the ridge levelled out; from this point we broke off to the left down a long slope. This would bring us quickly down to the corrie in the Blaven horse-shoe, a place where we should be sheltered from the wind and within easy reach of the point on Loch Slapin where we had left the car. The wind had been at our backs when we started to gain the ridge; it had blown side-on to us during the actual traverse, and now it was blowing in our faces. This diabolical arrangement ensured that every weakness in our garments was penetrated by rain! The salt tang in the wind was now very noticable and stung our cheeks and tasted on our lips.

The gentle slope, free of rocks or heather, lent a certain ease and speed to descent and the more vigorous motion brought the heat slowly back to our limbs.

Yet the slope seemed unending. It felt as though hours had passed since we turned abruptly at the col and faced into the wind. And the wind itself—that was a funny thing! I judged that we should be lower than the corrie walls and thus protected in a small measure from its full blast: but it was not diminished and the curious salty tang grew stronger.

"You don't think——," I began, and checked myself for even mentioning it.

Down we went. The slope was of a uniform angle, smooth and made comfortable going. That was the mysterious part of it. Had we been tardily decending rough ground we should not have wondered at the lapse of time. But we were literally racing downwards in order to be clear of the hill before dusk, and still the misty grey hillslope stretched away before us.

And still we went down. What was it I heard? Was it the roar of breakers on some misty beach? I could not be sure, for voices were murmuring in my ears—the voices of tiredness which always repeat the same thing, a snatch of song, perhaps, or some silly phrase. I was exhausted and could have rolled into the heather there and then and slept.

My friend observed that we must have descended at least two thousand feet. I considered that it had been more. How low the mist was! Suddenly I heard the murmur of a stream. It reassured us to a considerable extent, for we had noticed a stream in this corrie on our ascent earlier in the day, though how long ago it seemed now!

The mist began to break and the ground ahead of us grow clearer and, as we went lower, the visible area enlarged. At last the curtain was lifted completely. I stopped and gazed. What had happened? There was no Loch Slapin, no road, no car; in their stead, there was sea—miles of it—and in the middle-distance fell a jutting black headland, crowned with cloud.

"Where? Why? How?"—the words tumbled from me incoherently.

My friend looked very grim about it and it was obvious to me that he knew the truth and was merely confirming it with observation. He examined the sea-cliffs and the headland and the curve of the bay beneath us.

"Where are we?" I asked more calmly.

"Camasunary Bay. We are on the wrong side of Blaven and miles away from anywhere! We must make for Elgol and see if someone will hire us a car there."

"Where's Elgol?" I enquired, without much interest.

His hand described a wide circle and his fingertip alighted in line with a head-land, the last of a score; mist-crowned and remote beyond words.

"There!" he said.

I shuddered!

Before committing ourselves irrevocably to the passage of the sea coast which would lead us to Elgol, we sought vainly for a less exhausting alternative. In the midst of our deliberations one of us noticed a tiny croft in the middle of the foreshore. It seemed as if smoke were coming from a chimney and this evidence of life in a place which we had given up as deserted was a cheerful omen. No matter how bad a situation looks an additional opinion is never unwelcome.

The person who came to the door, however, in answer to our repeated knock, was not of a co-operative turn of mind. In the first place he assumed a Crusoe-like attitude upon seeing two of his own kind, and we almost had to assure him that we were real and not possible figments of his imagination, (strained to the utmost by solitude). Then his conversation became merely repetitional, and he told us nothing beyond what we already knew. When asked by my friend if Elgol was the nearest village he repeated the sentence in an inverted form, turning it from a question into a statement of melancholy fact. And when we enquired if there was any other way of reaching this remote place, other than by the coast he became confused and shuffled his feet: confusion gave way to sullen silence and, wondering how we had offended, we stole away.

"I suppose we should have told him about the Great War!" said my friend, as we made for the cliffs.

To dwell in too much detail upon the journey which followed would not embellish this narrative. So tired was I that cliffs, path and grey stormy sea slipped by as in a lingering dream. We always seemed to be climbing, though we were never very far from the water. I do not think that the distance is much more than four or five miles: the path, however, is seldom level but clings diabolically to every irregularity on the coast, winding to the top of head-lands and dropping deeply into coves. In addition to this it was often necessary to climb above the path when a stream was unfordable in the usual place. At last Elgol became visible. Rain was falling heavily and the sad night was thickening upon the mountains across the bay.

"Now for a car," said my friend, as we strode into the village.

The person to whom we were directed shrugged his shoulders.

"Perhaps," he said slowly, "she will go, but I cannot be certain. It is not lately she has gone, but I will go and try her for you."

We followed him to a tumble-down shed and watched him open a large door: then "she" was brought to light. We had not anticipated that "she" would be a young car. This object, however, was something quite beyond the range of our most pessimistic imaginings. It was fantastic and, under other circumstances, would have been laughable, for whilst the broad essentials of a car, the wheels (so far as I could see), the chassis, the body, were all present—beyond this the resemblance ceased. The whole had plainly been put together by an enthusiastic—but unskilled—amateur. The doors did not fit the doorways, the rear wheels were not of the same circumference, and the engine was constructed under a bonnet far too small to cover it.

Its master approached it. I think that we were both of the opinion that he was about to begin incantations, for we were now convinced that magic alone would produce the required results. Instead he gripped the starting handle: on the first turn a loud rattling complaint came from the engine in whose interior the confusion must have been intense, and he then lifted a door out, climbed inside and made some curious motions with a screw driver. He then returned to the handle.

"Perhaps, she will go now," he said unsmilingly.

He turned the handle—there was a loud bang!

We both jumped for we had not expected any reaction at all, but it was no cause for optimism. This was not the healthy and controlled back-fire of a normal car but an undesired explosion within the engine which probably completed the destruction of it.

We left him exhorting "her" in passionate Gaelic phrases. There was nothing for it but to take to the road. Within fifteen minutes a little car, driven by a friendly clergyman, picked us up. I sat in the back listening to the purring of the engine and comparing it with the queer noises at Elgol. We must have gone some miles before fate let loose another shaft against us. This time it came in the shape of a large motor lorry, carelessly driven, which collided with us sufficiently to send us into the ditch.

"By God's Grace we have escaped injury or death," said the clergyman, and we echoed the phrase with a wider implication. Strong—and very willing—hands raised the little vehicle to the road, and once again we set off.

Twenty minutes later we were in my friend's car racing back to Sligachan.

How wonderful it is to sleep after a long day on the hills, when tired limbs sink into the bedclothes and the mind into peaceful oblivion!

Our Skye holiday ended—the one I have written about here—years ago: but each day of its adventures are as clear now as when they occurred. I find it sad to think that this little strip of remembered time is surrounded before and after by hundreds of unrecollected days. I often think about this hill life, and compare its joys with other joys, and such sadness as belongs to it I have compared with other sadnesses. And I can frankly say:—these early Skye days are invested with the bright colour of memory that invests all youthful experience, and yet there is more to it than that: for they are not *merely* experiences, they represent a way of life; and this way of life is one to whose promptings I will listen as long as there is breath in my body.

A Song FOR the MORNING

The GRay Castle

My left foot sank deeply in the soft, moist peat. I drew it out with a quick movement and it reappeared with a curious sucking noise. The right foot, insecurely balanced, also became involved and was lost to sight. I briefly consigned the entire moorland to a region where its bogs would be expected to lose their offending moisture, and floundered helplessly. Norman, who was cautiously navigating the quaking ground by means of such stones and roots as seemed to offer a secure footing, turned round to smile at me and, seeing my plight, slung the end of a climbing rope towards me. I grasped it and with a strong effort shook off the insidious grip of the mud.

The country around us was barren in the extreme and typical of many northern and westerly Scottish regions. Flat, green hollows, filled with waterlogged peat, were interlaced by craggy ridges and tiny lochs. For as far as the eye could see this combination was the order of the moorland, although not always arranged in the same way. Here you would find a tiny lake placed high on the shoulder of a ridge in such a manner as to arouse your amazement at the way the waters were retained there. Then again, and more logically, a deep hollow would hold another reedy pond. A stretch of peat nearby would support a heathery rock-crowned ridge. Always they were there, these three essential features of the waste—the craggy rise, the quaking bog, the still and lifeless pond—but never were they in the same relationship to one another.

THE GRAY CASTLE

I have said that this country was typical of much of the land which makes up the north and west, but in so doing I was only referring to the immediate terrain, the characteristics of which I have just described. The skyline was very significant, and one glance would confirm a guess as to its whereabouts. Some two miles ahead the moor had been caught between a titanic finger and thumb, drawn up to a great height, the heather and moss stripped from the sides of the fold thus formed, the top of the hump flattened and pressed down far enough to cause the sides to bulge—and, I suppose, set like that as a reminder of the one-time mutability of the earth's surface. A sandstone hay-stack! A giant's castle built of solid rock! One look at it, and he who is sensitive to mountain visions, when he has finished shouting with a kind of joy, will surely roar with laughter—the Gray Castle! To be sure, the Stack to the south is a yet more fantastic place, but it is smaller and slimmer, and although its summit ridge rises from the moors like the back of a gigantic lizard it does not strike the eye with the same force of impact as the Gray Castle. The Stack *might* be a dream: the Gray Castle, heavy, sudden, still and sustained, could only be reality.

As Norman and I approached we kept glancing at it. We had set our hearts on breaching the line of rocky fortifications and scaling the front of the tower. From the sea, five miles away, one could speak lightly and optimistically about the gray patch of precipice that stood up out of the moor. Now our intentions and its proximity compelled attention. We seated ourselves upon a rock and considered the problem before us.

The angle on the north side was not quite as steep as that on the south. There seemed to be a great deal of lank grass and heather investing the slabs of rock on either flank, and, in addition, those to the south were glistening with water. Immediately above us a great sheet of rock, too bare for vegetation of any kind, was demarcated sharply by a long, shallow gully of what looked like mud and grass. These, broadly speaking, were the features of the great face that now stood close above us and which was so steep that even at this proximity, there was little or no foreshortening.

We discussed the various possibilities as they occurred to us, and our first choice was the great central slab of bare rock. We had no liking for grass that grew on steep rock faces and on that particular section there was none visible. We had noticed that the rock on the small ridges we had crossed was well fissured, but rounded and more likely to provide good footholds and ledges than good handholds. We had a small meal of sandwiches and coffee on the strength of our decision, rested for a few moments, and then started to climb the steep grass slope that led to the crags. The day was a gray one, dry but threatening.

A terrace of sandstone ran round the mountain beneath the start of the cliff. This was about forty feet in height and gave us some idea of the nature of the climbing. We went up a vertical wall, along a rising traverse and round some wet, slimy corners. and found ourselves on a wide ledge beneath the precipice itself. The mud gully was to the right. The slab, now seen as a buttress, rose alongside it. It only needed a glance to tell us that on this the climbing, if any, was to be found. It was a fine face of sandstone, broken but not dangerously shattered, with what appeared to be wide square ledges for a good deal of its height. It was impossible to assess much of the quality of the cliff from a climbing viewpoint as we were directly beneath and our vision of it was hopelessly distorted. One feature only was apparent from here which had been invisible from the place where we had eaten our sandwiches. It was a band of rock, set very steeply, which ran round the entire face at a height of about two hundred feet.

We roped together on the grass beneath the first ledge. I was acutely conscious of the sense of strain, with which anyone who has undertaken an unfamiliar climb will be aquainted. This was not going to be easy. I was also aware that if we were successful it would be a climb of no small merit, and the two feelings—fear and enthusiasm—combined to key me up for the task ahead.

"All ready?" asked Norman cheerfully. "This is going to be *some* climb. Give me a couple of shouts when you find a decent ledge and, in case I'm asleep, tug the rope! Good luck to you!"

I swung away on small holds and climbed steeply up to the first ledge. This was formed by the floor of a recess and was arched over by a roof of sandstone. There was no progress to be made in this direction but to the left a second ledge commenced. Between them there was a smooth surface of rock and one small foothold.

"Gymnastics begin," I shouted to Norman, "here one does the trapeze act without the trapeze. If I jump across this gap, is there any way down on the other side—supposing I can't go higher?" I waited while he walked round the base of the buttress.

"Yes," came his answer, "you can follow a traverse down again. Why don't you go up this way? If you miss the other ledge you'll get banged about on these rocks," and he indicated a pile of scree some twenty feet below me.

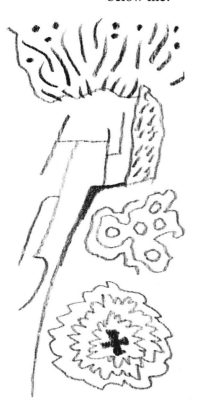

"It's not far," I answered, doubtfully, "too much trouble to come down. I'll risk it." Without giving my waning nerve time to go completely I drew in some slack rope and sprang into space. For what seemed a matter of moments I was quite convinced that I was going to overshoot, but no, my feet landed fair and square on a flat surface.

Recovering from the effort, I looked about me. To my left there was a further ledge but it was practically joined to the one on which I stood, while to my right a rather smooth ten foot wall would have conveyed me to the over-hanging roof of the first ledge. I decided to investigate to the left before I undertook the ascent of the wall and walked over to the second ledge after having aquainted Norman with my intentions.

From the far corner of the ledge a savage sight burst upon me. The crag projected at the point upon which I stood and from it the tremendous sweep of the northern precipice was visible. Though hardly so steep as the frontal buttress it appeared much longer. What really engrossed my interest was a tiny ledge, continuous with one upon which I stood, that wound across the face for a hundred yards or more. It was the kind of place upon which charlatan writers of mountaineering stories in boy's magazines love to place their determined heroes, but it was not for me. What made this latter fact so exasperating was that beyond the ledge the sweep of the buttress was broken up and distinctly promising. "I won't try," I said to myself, "if I got halfway across that I'd never get back! "

So I returned to the wall on the right of the first ledge. Here it soon became obvious there was not the slightest chance of success in this direction. Very much subdued I followed the course Norman had indicated and presently stood beside him.

"Your turn,"I said, "dashed if I can see anything feasible up there. There's a magnificent ledge, but—not much hope at all."

Norman quickly climbed up by my initial route, sprang across the gap with a roar of joy, and followed the two ledges to their conclusion at the beginning of the northern precipice. Here I heard him say something in a very excited manner, and he presently returned. "What a wonderful ledge," was his only comment.

We now began a close examination of every possible point of weakness in the great bastion of rock. At the end of two hours we were still in the same area. The afternoon was turning to evening when we at last decided to attack the only remaining alternative—the mud gully. Neither of us had any real desire to tackle this ostensibly dangerous route but it was the only way to the summit that our remaining time made possible. We roped at the bottom in a grim silence.

I led out the first hundred feet of the rope and began to look for some sort of stance. All round me was grass and heather clinging desperately to a slope of eighty degrees. Both my feet were slowly giving way but I had hold of two tufts of heather which seemed to be deeply rooted in what soil there was. There was clearly nowhere here to make a stance, so I climbed higher. At last, with Norman a hundred and twenty feet below me, my eyes alighted upon a shallow gash in the slope. I entered it and assumed a position of some security.

"Norman," I shouted, "there's a hole and I'm in it. You can come up here."

He joined me soon and his fingers were black where he had thrust them deeply into the soil. We looked above us. There was little to commend what we saw there. The slope continued at a uniform angle and was then crossed by a low wall of rock. Above this potential obstacle we could see no more so we judged that the slope must ease a little. To our left the buttress fell steeply towards the scene of our earlier attempts.

We climbed another two hundred feet in a similar manner. The grass and heather were firmer than we had expected and our only fear now was that the rock wall might stop our progress. I was ten feet below it when an accident nearly occurred: a piece of heather to which I had trusted my left hand came away with such suddenness that my balance was disturbed and my left foot dragged out of the hole which I had kicked for it, while all the weight of my body was transferred to my right hand and foot. The foothold promptly crumbled and I could feel the stump of heather in my hand dragging its roots. My feet were hopelessly placed and I could only kick them in the hope that they might engage in a hole which I had previously formed. In the nick of time I remembered a sound handhold I had used: it was low but would probably hold me when the moment came. I located it to the left of my waist and grasped it firmly. The heather then came away in my right hand and I sank slowly down against the resistance of the left arm. A moment later my feet engaged with holes.

It was a moment of great alarm and I rested a moment before returning to the wall. Norman had guessed what had happened but did not mention it at the time. The wall now assumed a more sinister aspect, for if I could not climb it I began to doubt my ability to return! In this I need have had no fears. The wall was a superb place. Hand and footholds were deeply cut and secure and I lingered on it for this reason, rejoicing in a sense of safety that I had not experienced since the beginning of the gully climb. Beyond it I saw that the angle was much reduced and the end of the climb at hand. Norman joined me in a small crevice just above the wall. A wide ledge took us easily from the gully to a point well out on the great central slab and we paused to enjoy a tremendous sense of exposure in this dramatic place.

The precipice above our heads was vertical and in places the rocks actually overhung. Examining this formidable barrier in the faint hope that there might be a line of weakness in it, we could see nothing beyond the final overhang and we both concluded that the angle beyond that point probably decreased; for we had climbed four or five hundred feet up the gully and must now be near to the summit of the Castle. The eye of faith, however, could make nothing of the intervening stretch.

Beginning to return from the ledge in a rather subdued frame of mind, Norman suddenly said,

"What about the camera?" and I appreciated what he meant at once.

"Why, perfect I should think!"

We returned to the end of the ledge and took up sensational postures at its extreme tip. First Norman was submitted to the photographic eye: then I, in my turn, was arranged for the best effect. The simple approach to the ledge was hidden: the rope was so arranged as to suggest that it was the decisive factor in a life or death struggle: a river far below had been thoughtfully included in the scene and utmost use made of the angle of all vertical rocks, with less severe slopes carefully excluded from the view. The result was astonishing, so much so indeed that on first seeing the photographs we were both compelled to look twice before being finally convinced: we saw ourselves in a position of intense difficulty from which it seemed only the most unusual skill could have released us, and we found it hard to reconcile this prospect with the reality we remembered, a ledge so wide that a blind man, with reasonable care, could have been led along it!

Upon retreating from our assumed positions and returning to the gully, there was nothing more to cause delay, for it rose at a reduced angle and our upward progress was fast. Within twenty minutes we stood by the substantial cairn on the summit of the Gray Castle.

This is a place where, if the mood were wrong, it might be terrible to be alone. A man could go mad in such a strange place devoid of the props that hold the mind in balance, for here one stands upon a rocky pillar that guards a long and lonely land, a land in which ten thousand ponds blink up at one like dead, white eyes. There is no sign of man from here, nor of any of his works, everything one sees from here precedes him; that is why the mind, be it not lashed tightly to the ordinary and usual, springs up and may gallop away upon the wild steed of fantasy. The top of the hill is like a bowl and drops away on every side. In one direction, not very far away, is the ridge which straggles up into a fantastic pinnacle.

Thus Norman and I, staying long enough to feel the spirit of the place, shouldered our packs and made off towards the straggling ridge.

Sunshine
and Storm

Mountains with equal attributes, like people whose qualities are similar, do not attract one equally. For ten years the great Cairngorm range, nearer and more readily accessible than any other group of hills, held very little appeal for me. I was not unaware of the vast, empty acres of Ben McDhui, nor of the beetling cliffs that hang above the Coire an Lochan: I had visited the gloomy Lairig, with its white, blinking eyes of pools and also the peace of the Rothiemurchus woods on a long summer afternoon. Even the hurricane blast on the confusing ridges of Cairn Toul were reasonably familiar from sporadic expeditions to them, but they did not exert the same fascination as the isolated ranges of the north and west or the fantastic island spires of Skye.

I cannot account for this prolonged failure to appreciate a very varied and wonderful range, and when at last it began to occur to me that here were rock faces of a very high standard and largely unexplored, I became quite upset: rocks held a greater attraction for me than mountains! I discovered some books about the Cairngorms and read them assiduously. Certain points stood out. The majority of the rock faces were very remote and only a few routes had been made upon them. The first fact explained the second. There was a mountain that could be reached by road, at least there was a road marked upon the map, but I doubted how far I might get upon it and in the end resolved to walk it and Norman, who was to be my companion on the expedition, decided to use a new pair of climbing boots for the occasion.

We set off from Coylum Bridge on a fine, midsummer's morning. The hills ahead of us were shrouded in a dark mist but, with the passing of each moment, this seemed to merge and vanish into the blue sky above it. The road was rough but well-graded and we strode merrily along. Norman was ostentatiously proud of his boots and drew my attention more than once to a sharply defined outline of new nails in the softer part of the track. Mine (to which he also drew attention) failed to disturb the smooth surface; those nails which had not worn away in prolonged conflict with rocks, had fallen out of the tired leather. As I pointed out to him however, since it was dry we should probably use our sandshoes on the rocks; the superior claims of his boots would not be exhibited this day! Mine, furthermore were comfortable.

We walked for an hour. At the end of that time we were rising above the last trees into a bare valley; to our left was a conical hill. Norman's right foot seemed to be giving him trouble and now and again, he snatched it from the ground as though the ground were hot. I made no comment. We walked on.

The morning had matured perfectly. The transitory dawn mist was gone from the summits. A shimmering haze hid the details of the further hills but revealed their outlines; their bulks were not decreased, but they seemed doubly distant and stood up in a kind of unassailable remoteness and my friend, now beginning to perform odd antics in the road, had reason to curse the diabolical conditions of visibility in which they were displayed.

Norman limped painfully along. Suddenly, at the top of a rise, we saw our mountain for the first time and in the mists of the warm morning it appeared to be ten miles away. The knowledge of the pain he had suffered was coupled for Norman with the expectation of agony to come, and he kicked his toes against a rock to reduce the pressure on his heels and remarked sadly, "I wish I hadn't bought these boots; they're killing me: I shall take them off and walk bare-foot. My sandshoes are too small—they would be worse!"

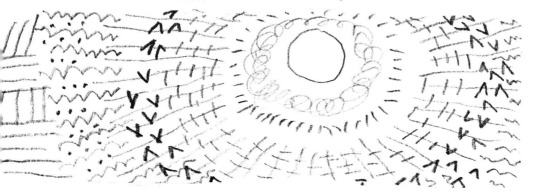

The road—at this point somewhat reduced in quality—ran near a boisterous stream in a valley through which glaciers had growled in ancient times. A few trees were still studded upon the slopes, but they were the vanguard in the war against wind and altitude. Ahead of us an enormous mountain squatted like a fabulous animal, and to its right, smaller and steeper, was the hill we had chosen for our objective.

We knew that on the side which would presently be facing us there were a series of rocky buttresses. We had intended to climb the last one, which lay furthest along the glen, but Norman's lacerated heel now caused us to curtail this plan, and we decided on the initial cliff.

My friend was remarkably cheerful during the next few miles. A bruised heel, no more than an annoying trifle in town-life, can easily ruin a day's enjoyment on the hills, but Norman's bounding humour was more than a match for anything of this kind and he turned his obvious discomfort into a source of amusement. The bare foot experiment was a failure: his attempts to anticipate the feel of a stone before he trod upon it were not always successful and cries of pain were mingled with shouts of laughter as he danced about each time he had the misfortune to place his foot on a sharp surface. As one can easily imagine, this mode of progression was slow and the sun was high in the heavens before we were even drawing near to the buttress. The haze had increased and the rocks were no more than shadowy gray outlines against a sky in which mountainous white clouds were beginning to assemble.

Leaving the road, we stumbled through the sun-warmed heather and climbed slowly up a slope towards the buttress. The heat was intense and there was not a stir of wind, but high overhead the building of the cloud castles silently continued. Far up the glen there was a long sparkling sheet of water and several times we had to resist the inclination to leave our attempt on the buttress to go and wallow in the cool waters. The hot toil of the climb up the heathery approach once over, however, the prospect of gray slabs of granite brought back our enthusiasm for the sterner pleasures of the climb. It was really a superb day for the rocks and we removed our boots gratefully and changed into sandshoes.

79

The buttress above us consisted of two roughly-shaped faces of rock divided by a cavernous gully. We wondered if this would yield a climb and glanced into its humid depths. But in the warm atmosphere of the summer's afternoon, there was something diabolical in the sombre reaches where the sun was a stranger and the eternal drip-drip of water made sad music. Norman, whose sun-browned face looked pale in the gloom, said suddenly,

"Let's get out of here, it might avalanche or something any minute. I don't like this place at all!"

Accordingly we examined the two buttresses on either hand. That to the south was steep, but, while much of its length was broken up into long sections of heather, it was crowned by a mighty rampart of gray, vertical rock the sight of which alarmed us. The northern buttress was longer, less steep and more continuously rocky. It was decided upon and at once we commenced to climb near the right-hand side of the gully. The rock was warm to the touch: we swarmed from ledge to ledge and gained height rapidly. The holds were ample and the surface rough, for the granite of the mountain was formed into terraces and between these were stretches of cliff. We took it in turns to lead these sections. During the passage of one of them, when about ten feet above a terrace, a piece of rock upon which my feet were resting moved suddenly and then gave way. My handholds were inadequate to take the unsupported weight of my body and, with a quick shout of warning to Norman (who was directly beneath me), I fell. No sooner was I clear of the rock face than an awful apprehension took hold of me. This fear was entirely unfounded, for reason told me that in no circumstances could I miss the broad terrace on which my friend was securely placed; but it persisted horribly until I made a clean landing on the shelf with both feet, rolled back from the edge, still six feet away, and into a clump of heather, to sit up facing my friend.

"I don't think this mountain would give you any second chances," he said quietly.

Although it was now utterly gone, I did not mention the sudden flash of fear to him for it seemed like cowardice (a very personal feeling of which few are keen to speak) in view of the absurdly small degree of danger that accompanied the incident. It was obvious, however, that we had assessed the quality of rock too highly, so from then on we advanced more cautiously.

The sky was now piled high with immense ramparts of cloud and the air was agitated by little gasps of warm wind. Neither of us liked the look of the weather and soon the necessity for speed—if we were to avoid a thunderstorm on the open face—became apparent. This clashed with our conviction that caution was necessary in view of the shaky condition of the rocks, and we compromised by unroping and climbing up a less exposed side of the buttress. At the time we both doubted the absolute wisdom of this step, but we were faced with the alternative of risking a sudden downpour which would drench the rocks and make climbing in plimsols a suicidal act. We had left our boots at the base of the cliff.

A few minutes later Norman directed my attention to something which confirmed our fears. Slowly advancing over the back of the mountain and apparently projecting from the ridge above our heads, was a dense black cloud of swirling vapours that seemed to be of the consistency of burning oil, and was moving with a determined yet stealthy motion. It was being driven like a wedge into the clear, untroubled atmosphere above, and the base of this wedge seemed to move at a greater speed than the apex, as though the air were offering resistance to its passage. We both looked grim but the irrepressible Norman managed a joke:

"If you've any iron in your pockets, throw it away !"

Within the next five minutes a great change came over the mountain. The light of day was gradually withdrawn and replaced by a dim radiance which seemed to rise from the earth rather than to descend from the sky. On the mountain itself, outstanding ridges were quickly eclipsed as local shadows suffered obliteration by the universal shadow now passing across the sky.

We climbed higher in silence, trying not to pay too much attention to the elemental devilry that was going on overhead, but expecting the thunder which we felt must come at any moment.

Another ten minutes went by. It had grown very dark and with the passage of each moment it grew darker. It was as though the hill had been invested by a separate night, for on the mountains beyond the fringe of the storm cloud the sun was still shining brightly. A hope entered my mind that the storm might cross the top of our mountain intact and break upon its loftier neighbour. I looked up, and the hope died. The activity in the cloud was tremendous; the base seemed to have stopped its forward motion altogether, while the apex was rushing on alone and immediately above us were swirling vortices of vapour, dark as night, some of which seemed to have made contact with the upper parts of the mountain. I turned to the climb again.

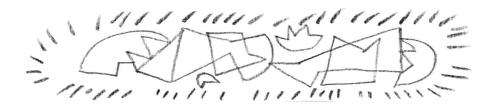

A light lit the world around, a light brighter than I have ever seen. It did not seem to flash with the unstable violence of ordinary lightning, but to hang and hover in the boiling clouds. For a long moment ridges stood out like iron, gullies like pits of jet, the shivering water of the loch flashed a reflective gleam, while the heather at our feet was shadowed on the slab. I flung myself down, and Norman did the same, for fear that the mountain had been struck above us and that in a moment the air would be filled with falling granite. All was quiet for a fraction of a second—and then the caverns of sound were opened, and out of the dark, whirling vortices of pandemonium above, came a volcano's subterranean voice when its irresistable breath has split the carcase of the earth asunder: no other sound, I am certain, could be compared to that thunderclap amid the mountains. No sooner had the first report rattled, than its echo was flung back upon us and in its reiterating roar I heard the crash of boulders falling from the mountain not far away from us. Indeed, when I raised my head, dust was rising like steam above the gully into whose depths great rocks were bounding from the shattered structure of a granite pinnacle.

Norman and I, with a single thought, scuttled into the shelter of an overhanging cave. Our future course could be decided later: at the moment, our prime consideration was to avoid the debris of another pinnacle which, at any time, might be struck and disintegrate higher up the mountain. No sooner were we under cover than a second flash was followed by another tremendous roar. This time, although the flash was neither so near nor so bright, it was accompanied by a distinct sizzling noise which made our blood run cold. No more rocks fell, however, and for this mercy we gave thanks.

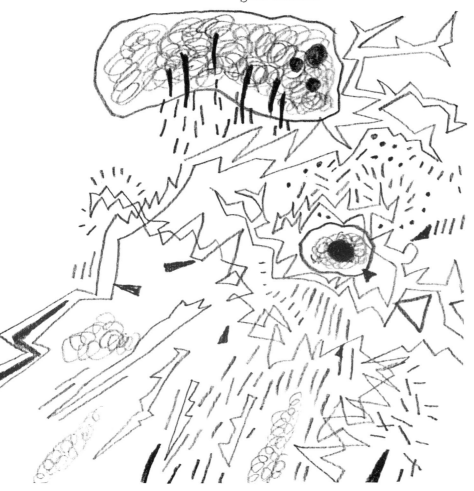

Within another five minutes the actual storm, heralded by those tremendous electrical discharges, broke opposite us upon the plateau of the four highest mountains. We watched the lightning flickering to earth and blazing from cloud to cloud. The thunder became incessant and periods between the explosions were occupied by their echoing passage from crag to crag. At the far end of the glen the dark clouds had become streaked with vertical lines of gray where the rain was falling upon the arid slopes. A huge drop splashed outside our shelter, then another and another. Soon a little rivulet formed down the concave top of an adjacent boulder.

There was nothing we could do now but wait. It was probable that the passing of the storm would bring a return of evening sunshine and if too much rain did not fall in the meantime there was a chance that the warm rocks might dry.

The crashing and booming on the plateau was fascinating to watch as the interplay of lightning amid the drifting dark clouds was staged, with the occasional lifting of a cloud to reveal the outline of a rain-lashed ridge. The gray stain was spreading slowly across the low sky. Slowly the downpour increased and from the mountains began to emanate the most delicate of all scents: the sweet breath of rain's union with warm earth. We soon abandoned all hope of dry rocks and even an early escape from our position. From my seat in the cave I could just see, far down the slope, the steep wall of the gully. Beyond it rose the tremendous cliff of the rampart, from which water was now spurting in numerous and sudden cascades, that a few minutes before had been utterly motionless and in ancient silence; now the intense activity of the streams produced an illusion of one concerted movement, whose voices were raised in tumultous music. The thunder clouds streaming over the high crags also gave the impression that the mountain itself was in motion rather than the clouds. Only on the last of the buttresses an enormous pinnacle defied the efforts of the storm to submerge it and stood coldly up in the turbulent mists like the accusing finger of Justice amid the ebb and flow of human misdemeanour.

A wind now began to rise and whip the rain against the cliff from every conceivable direction. The shelter was far from waterproof and very soon its walls were streaming with moisture. Instead of the early improvement for which we had hoped the storm, as far as we could judge from our limited viewpoint, showed no signs of abating. We discussed what we should do. Norman was keen for an immediate attempt on the summit, but I was very doubtful in view of the amount of water coming down the slabs: in sandshoes the proposal seemed a hazardous one, even though mountain streams dry up with the same remarkable suddeness with which they commence. I still hoped for a miraculous change in conditions.

We waited for fifteen minutes. Then I rose and went out: the rain lashed against me and the wind sang in my ears. I glanced up at the slabs; water was streaming down them, rushing and gurgling, and at cracks and ledges spouting out into the air. As the wind ripped around, it caught the descending torrents, twisted them, and sent them backwards in sheets of spray. I returned to Norman with a face of excessive length.

"We'll never get up there in rubbers," I remarked, "it's like a river."

"Oh, well, and we can't stay here. Nothing for it, it'll have to be stockings. My blinking best climbing pair, too!"

"Bad luck. Want to lead?"

"Not in the least, but to oblige a friend—"

The gloom produced by the storm was being replaced by the true darkness of approaching night. We left the cave and stood beneath the initial slab, and waves of spray were blown up in our faces. We removed the sand-shoes and put on the rope. Norman made an attempt to gain a footing on the commencement of a slab. He had climbed for about three feet when a gush of water, twisted by the wind, dashed against his face and detroyed his balance; and he let go and landed beside me.

"This is *some* game," he shouted, above the wind.

He tried again. This time he overcame the short stretch of vertical rock and established himself on easier slabs. The water attacked him savagely, for the place he had chosen, though less steep than any other section of the ridge above us, was more subject to the watery effects of the storm. It was a concavity between two outstanding ridges and was acting as a natural drainpipe. An irrelevant sound became audible to me and, after a moment of puzzlement, I realised that my friend was roaring with laughter in sheer joy at his unusual struggle.

The streams of water were breaking against his hands and running up his sleeves to cascade finally from his elbow. He seemed to find great amusement in the business, and indeed I cannot remember an occasion drab, dangerous or unpleasant that was able to stifle his merriment. His nature was one of those to which all life's hazards were things of joy and all its crudities objects of interest and speculation, for he was born with an optimism which he flourished like a banner. He and I had climbed together since we were no more than children, and never have I seen him reduced to that cold, white and desperate mood wherein so many other brave men seek the pinnacle of their courage.

Now he seated himself behind a jutting rock and shouted to me to come up. I flung myself upon a rock and grappled mightily with it, plunging my hands into water two or three inches deep in order to grasp submerged holds. The water crept insidiously up my sleeves, and presently I felt its cold touch upon my shoulders. Care was sacrificed on the altar of speed and, in the full knowledge of the rope round my waist, I rushed up the slabs. Upon reaching the point where Norman was seated I cried out to him:

"If you don't mind I'll lead on, for I'll suffer if I sit down. As soon as I'm entirely wet I'll be all right."

This was true: there are no worse moments than those in which the last few stitches are being inundated and there was not long to wait before the required conditions were met. A stream, frothing down between two ridges gave me the *coup de grace*: I misjudged a submerged foothold and went flat on my face into the water, and on regaining my feet I experienced a sense of physical well-being accompanied by mental jubilation. Norman climbed up to me and led on in his turn.

In this mad, jolly, irresponsible fashion we reached the crest of the ridge just as the retreating pennons of the storm rose above the summit of the mountain and drew majestically away. We seated ourselves on a small boulder and built a cairn. At the time we believed this to be a first ascent but, as transpired subsequently, it had been climbed once before.

Opposite us, across the gully, there was a preciptious wall of rock. Norman was looking hard at it.

"Is that a climber?" he asked me, pointing to a small shape in the middle of the cliff.

"Surely not," I replied, "it isn't moving." He looked for a moment or two longer before saying,

"No. I suppose not. What a sinister looking place!"

We rose then and walked up the steep slope that ended in the summit of the mountain under a sky purged and purified by rain. The storm had expended its full fury upon the neighbouring hills and now only long tatters of cloud were fleeing towards the east, the remnants of a retreating army.

We reached the cairn and carried out an old custom which had been ours since boyhood; we climbed up each side of the cairn and shook hands across it. Then we sat down and marvelled at the beauty of the evening, for the sun was just setting beneath the horizon, but in the azure sky there was a white aura of light against which distant mountains were drawn in black marbled outlines.

On the enormous plateau opposite the colours defied description. The fading light had robbed the russet moorland of its warmth and the heathery slopes were now wrapped in a sombre brown making the rocky summits, of a much lighter hue, float upon their darkening bases.

We waited until the remaining light had withdrawn into a small area in the corner of the western sky. Then with the evening turning to night, we realised we were drenched to the skin. We dashed down the steep hillside between buttresses that were now traced darkly against the sky and sought for the place where we had left our boots. For fifteen minutes we conducted a fruitless search.

"Norman," said I with growing alarm, "was it in this stream or that?"

"That!" he replied.

When we had taken the decision to leave our boots, the safest place seemed to be in the bed of a dried up stream. This arbitrary assumption had led us into desperate straits, for now the water was a foot deep and the boots gone. All we could do was to follow the course of the stream and hope against hope that they had lodged somewhere, and that we should come across them before absolute darkness made further search impossible. We walked slowly downwards and examined each pool carefully as we came to it. For a long time our efforts were unrewarded and we became more thorough as our pessimism grew. Suddenly I saw a dark, familiar shape lying deeply in a heather-fringed pool. I gave a shout of triumph:

"Here's one. The others can't be far!"

"Why can't they? Is it one of yours or mine? Yours? Pity, they aren't much use to me."

Within five minutes we had rounded them all up and were occupied in the revolting task of substituting soaking shoes for soaking boots. Stars were beginning to flicker in a sky from which all clouds were gone before we reached the beginning of the road. Here Norman sat down and drew a pen-knife from his pocket. I watched him in fascinated silence as he began to undertake radical alterations to his right boot, cutting and hacking in grim determination, as though he were performing vengeance upon the body of an enemy who had done him great evil.

"That's better," he remarked, as he removed the offending portion of the heel and flung it away into the heather.

The mountain was far blacker than the night as we took our last glance at it from the place where it had first appeared twelve hours before. Massive and incredibly strong it stood there, unflattered by the sunshine, undaunted by the storm, a terrible antagonist. Norman was still looking at it as we turned to the last long miles of our return journey. My mind was now centred doggedly upon the means of relieving a dreadful hunger, but my friend's thoughts were concerned with the hill. He said something which was inaudible to me and I asked him what it was.

"That's a treacherous mountain!" he repeated almost under his breath, and gave a little laugh to show that he did not want me to take him too seriously.

INSIDE THE MOUNTAIN

A friend said to me once during a mountaineer's gathering at Glen More Lodge, "See what you think about the long crack in the buttress above the Red Slab." Some hours later three of us were cutting steps in the steep snow below the crest of Cairn Lochan (near Cairn Gorm), and so intent was I on finding a possible route through the cornices that it escaped my memory. Also, the demoralising sight of huge masses of fractured snow hanging over our heads struck a degree of terror into our hearts. We paused to think, and the sum of each of our thoughts was identical—retreat or perish! Being young men, and entertaining a due regard for the sacredness of human life, we undertook the former alternative; and so it was on the way down that my friend's words came into my mind and I glanced at the cliff opposite, in the hope of seeing the crack in question. There was no very obvious route: the granite rocks were set at a forbidding angle.

"Do you see anything like a crack there?" I shouted to Kenneth, who was climbing above me. He scanned the crag and replied,

"Yes, in the middle of the buttress, filled with snow. It's a long, narrow slit. I can just see a chockstone blocking it near the top. I can't see a way in, though, or any route over the stone. Looks pretty interesting: we must come back on a warmer day and try—" but his last words were carried away appropriately on a blast of icy wind. We had no further opportunity of discussing the crack, and very little for looking at it, for a sudden snow shower of blizzard force had risen and was howling against the plateau. All our attention was given to getting down in safety.

During the passage of the next few months we did not forget about the crack, but the winter was severe and the fissure is not far from the four thousand foot line, and it was obvious that any attempt to climb it must be subject to the advent of a warm spell. Late spring brought the weather we required and early summer continued the good work. One day, from a hill above the Farm, Kenneth and I surveyed the dawn-flushed Cairngorms, and it was obvious that the time had come. We turned to each other and said in one voice, "Now for the Crack!"

It took a week or so to arrange a trip to Loch Morlich, but when it came we soon realised that we had been fortunate in our choice of day. The sky was clear, the wind brisk but warm, the ground underfoot dry and cracked from an unusual spell of sunshine. We arrived early at Glen More Lodge and shouldered our light packs once more. We were a party of four, but two members were intent upon climbing Cairn Gorm itself: we walked the first mile together until our friends branched off on the path up their mountain, while Kenneth and I remained on the track that aimed at the heart of Coire an Lochan.

A great mountaineer once remarked to me that seldom does one come across such compact scenery as in the Cairngorms and variety is certainly a conspicuous attraction of the five miles between the Lodge and the small loch in Coire an Lochan. Kenneth and I passed through a widely diverse pageant of natural beauty: the blue loch with its strand of bright, yellow sand; the strip of woodland glade and the narrow valley with its chattering river; and then the long, empty sweep of the moorland, and, crowning all, the desolate and devastated crags. We climbed quickly through the lower country and soon exchanged its vernal warmth for the cold austerity of the rock-girt corrie. Clambering over a wilderness of boulders and circumventing the tiny loch, we climbed the steep slope above it, where the weather was very fine but the wind had increased.

The Red Slab, which now reared up above us, is a unique feature of the corrie. I do not know of anything to equal it in Scotland. It is a mighty sheet of polished granite, set at a low angle, and of a distinct, ruddy colour. It cannot be easily regarded either as a prolongation of the cliffs downwards or as an upward addition to the corrie floor. In dry weather it is a joy to climb or, more accurately, to climb upon, for one can scuttle all over its surface by means of tiny cracks and ledges. In rain, a little more caution is demanded, but even then it is a joyous matter. Kenneth and I scampered over it with the verve and carelessness of March hares: and suddenly the sight of the crack burst upon us. We became motionless, balancing on dainty holds.

Hanging above our heads was a wall of rock of impressive proportion. It was vertical all the way up and arched with an audacious flourish above the angle of the slab. So steep was it, indeed, that the rock to which we clung, itself of no mean angle, seemed like a level floor beneath it. In places it was undercut where outraged gravity had taken a terrible revenge. And, in its steepest part, desperately remote, was a long, thin crack. It might have been four hundred feet in height, or more. It was certainly not much less. It appeared to be very deeply cut in places and to penetrate into the depths of the mountain. We sat down, regarding it critically, and in a few moments sandwiches and a flask of coffee had appeared. Kenneth was the first to break the involuntary silence. His remarks are usually apt, intelligent and original in the extreme, yet now, being stunned by the ferocious look of the place, he uttered a euphemism: "It doesn't look easy!"

Within fifteen minutes we had summed up two obvious problems. The entrance to the crack would give us trouble; it was very narrow and steep but not deeply-cut like the upper reaches. If we managed to surmount this section, a huge jammed stone might bring us to a halt. Beyond this it was not possible to surmise.

Sandwiches and coffee disposed of, we left the boots and haversacks together and donned plimsols. The ground beneath the crack was moist and mossy. "If we do come off, the ground is very soft!" I said, and forced a shallow smile. The nervous strain, always present at the start of a new (or severe) climb, was with us both. Kenneth gave me a tolerant glance and without more ado I commenced to grapple.

The entrance to the crack was about twenty foot from the ground, and easy climbing on rather shaky holds soon brought me level with it. It was even narrower and shallower than I had thought. I slipped my left arm inside and scraped about for a while. There were some small ledges on the left hand wall, and I grasped one of them and tried to lift myself high enough to insert my leg in the crack. It would not fit and I made an ungracious comment upon my leg being too large. My words did not improve the situation and the effort of uttering them left me weak and gasping. For the next five minutes I regaled my friend below with an account of how matters were going, though the verbal pattern of my failure indicated my rejection of the hold, and a frenzied scraping accompanied my search for a more propitious support. Kenneth, below, was becoming a little restive and several times expressed his surprise that I did not attempt to reverse my position in the crack. On the third reiteration of this sage advice I twisted my neck violently and gazed down at him.

"I told you, my foot is *stuck*," I said fiercely, "and what do you think of *that*?" Kenneth, seeing that my predicament made movement at the waist impossible, replied unhelpfully: "Perhaps you can untie your shoe!"

During the latter part of this banter my foot came free of its own accord, and I turned round. This greatly improved matters as I was now in a position to climb about ten feet. Here a small jammed stone offered a further problem. At the entrance to the crack I had been in an awkward position but it had been a safe one. Now, however, the situation was exposed and dangerous. There was a drop of thirty feet beneath, and it was not possible to assess the security of the jammed stone until I had relinquished a number of important holds.

In order to give me more moral and physical support I asked Kenneth if he would climb up to the start of the crack before I undertook the passage of the stone. He did so at once and I felt more confident.

It is an accepted maxim in climbing that it is not good to pull the body vertically upwards while the feet are left free to kick loose stones into ones comrades' faces. There are, of course, certain exceptions to this rule, and here was one of them. To overcome the jammed stone (having satisfied myself that it was reasonably secure) I put both hands over it, relinquished my footholds—not without misgivings—and pulled. My body rose up over the stone like an angelic soul triumphing over the evils of the world,

and my face was soon pressed into the dirt and soil behind the small boulder. Oblivious for the moment of the discomfort, I was only too glad to find that the stone had not failed me. A frenzied wriggle completed the movement which would obviously present a terrible problem in reverse.

"Come on!" I spluttered, ejecting pieces of mud and stone in the direction of my friend, "This is not so bad but you'll only need a one-way ticket for it." Kenneth climbed steadily up to me but found the passage of the stone possible only by the method I had used. We stood together on the small ledge and looked around. It was a fantastic place.

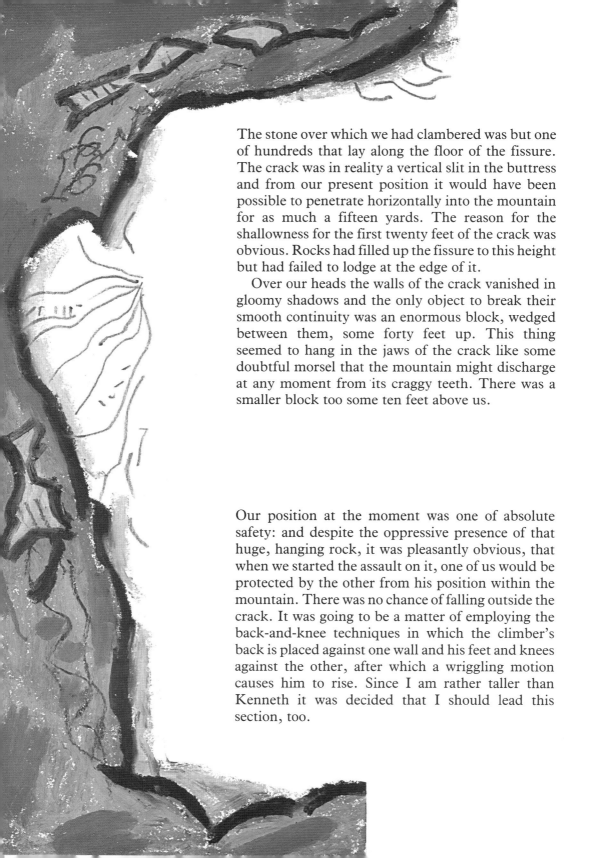

The stone over which we had clambered was but one of hundreds that lay along the floor of the fissure. The crack was in reality a vertical slit in the buttress and from our present position it would have been possible to penetrate horizontally into the mountain for as much a fifteen yards. The reason for the shallowness for the first twenty feet of the crack was obvious. Rocks had filled up the fissure to this height but had failed to lodge at the edge of it.

Over our heads the walls of the crack vanished in gloomy shadows and the only object to break their smooth continuity was an enormous block, wedged between them, some forty feet up. This thing seemed to hang in the jaws of the crack like some doubtful morsel that the mountain might discharge at any moment from its craggy teeth. There was a smaller block too some ten feet above us.

Our position at the moment was one of absolute safety: and despite the oppressive presence of that huge, hanging rock, it was pleasantly obvious, that when we started the assault on it, one of us would be protected by the other from his position within the mountain. There was no chance of falling outside the crack. It was going to be a matter of employing the back-and-knee techniques in which the climber's back is placed against one wall and his feet and knees against the other, after which a wriggling motion causes him to rise. Since I am rather taller than Kenneth it was decided that I should lead this section, too.

I climbed onto the top of the smaller block, and then Kenneth took himself into the dim and echoing shadows within the buttress. Starting about five feet in from the edge of the crack, I began to shuffle upwards. The only good holds, provokingly enough, were to be found near the edge, on approaching which I was treated to a view of the corrie which was nothing if not sensational. It was *directly* beneath me: the rocks were vertical. My progress was steady enough and, ten minutes after leaving Kenneth, I was thirty feet above him. The chockstone was now very near: it lay between me and the light which filtered through the walls of the crack. It was square-cut and its base was like a roof to the outer part of this craggy chamber.

In the gloom of the interior I could not be sure that the stone, huge and permanent as it looked, was securely held in position. Very often, ledges which arrest its vertical fall, will not hold a boulder if they be pushed sideways, and sometimes the balance of even the largest stones can be destroyed with alarming ease. I felt like a fish, desperate with hunger, who feels that his bait may be poisoned. I reached for a knob of rock on the side of the stone and gingerly applied light pressure. It was perfectly steady. I banged it with my shoulder. Not a tremor. Kenneth was watching me intently and at my second movement to test the stone's security he shouted up to me—"Tell me when you're going to throw it down, won't you?"

The problem now was to get on top of it. I have pointed out that the walls of the crack were broken up into good holds only at their external edges. This meant that the chockstone was placed directly over my only means of reaching it. To climb around the stone on the outside seemed to invite disaster, to go inside—one glance at the walls, smooth as marble, told me that this would be a struggle in which every square inch of adhesiveness that I possessed would be employed. It was by far the safest way, however, for by choosing it rather than the outside passage of the stone I should remain under Kenneth's control. I told him I intended to back-and-knee between the walls of the crack.

I waited on two good holds to muster up my strength for the coming effort. I examined the walls for holds; there was a tiny continuous cleft, hardly more definite than a scratch, which seemed to lead about ten feet into the crack. This was on the left wall so I placed my back against the right and began to wriggle. The problem was essentially one of pressure. A certain degree had to be maintained in order to keep me from sliding down but this had not to be so great as to prevent a lateral movement. In ten minutes I had moved ten inches. The little cleft was serving me well but my toes were tiring under the strain; in order to cut short the discomfort I moved more quickly and in so doing upset the carefully adjusted pressure. My back, which had not yet been brought into line with my feet, began to slip. A chill of horror shot through me: I was turning upside down! I uttered a loud shout. Quick as an explosion that follows a bullet from a gun's mouth came the answer to my shout: the rope snatched at me and restored my body to the perpendicular. Kenneth had been superbly alert.

"Thanks, friend," I said as calmly as possible, "remind me to do the same for you sometime," I paused to look, and then added, "I think that's done it!" Indeed it looked as though our efforts were about to be rewarded. The stone was now above my left shoulder: the side facing me was broken into crevices. With my left hand in one of these holds I steadied my movements and was soon on a level with the top of it, a quick sideways slide and the thing was under my feet. A feeling of enormous elation filled me and I called down to Kenneth, "Wonderful. That's a terrific climb. We must finish the crack now, whatever's above!"

Kenneth commenced to climb and approached steadily. He found the traverse beneath the stone awkward but performed it without faltering.

We now found ourselves in a very high and lonely place, a little harbour of safety on the vast face of the precipice. Standing on the chockstone, we felt the full sense of exposure: for it was as though we stood upon a bridge over the tremendous drop. Above us there was no obvious problem, for the crack was wider, shallower and much less steep. We were immensely pleased with ourselves and only tempered our pleaure with the knowledge that there *might* be some unknown barrier above us. In consequence, we did not linger long but set out to dispel the mysteries beyond.

We found nothing further to stop us. I ran out sixty or seventy feet of rope on moderate climbing over steep and sensational rocks. Quite suddenly it became apparent that the climb was coming to an end: the angle ceased, the rocks became broken, and very shortly I found myself on a square pinnacle of rock—separated from the rough summit of Cairn Lochan only by the summit of the fissure up whose eastern side we had climbed. When Kenneth had joined me we built a large cairn of stones to mark the top of the climb: it is there, I believe, to this day.

We now experienced that blending of relief and triumph which is one of the mountaineer's rewards for a long period of hard work. We looked across the corrie and followed with our eyes the route up which we had come. In the distant Spey valley we saw the tiny trail of smoke from a train going to the south. I thought of the numerous people in that train who, in their most extravagant dreams, would not think of having done what we had done this day: we sat with folded legs and inflated souls like two gods round our little altar.

Presently one of us suggested that, since it was still early, we should walk on to Ben McDhui. This mountain was little more than two miles away over an undulating plateau and after the rather limited—albeit strenuous—activity in the crack the idea of a brisk walk appealed. We crossed the top of the fissure and climbed easy rocks on to the top of Cairn Lochan.

The day had deteriorated considerably. Gone were the blue skies: the wind had risen to a fitful gale; the high summits were darkening. We hastened along in the direction of the twin grey hills of McDhui. It is quite impossible to cross these vacant spaces without allowing one's mind to revert to the Grey Man, that sizable spectre which is reputed to stride across the arid acres. It is variously reported as a massive shape, as the slow thud of footfalls in the mist, as a roaring voice complaining in uncouth Gaelic, or as music by the Pools of Dee in the high noon. I think it is a flash of fear which takes so many forms. The summits slopes of Ben McDhui are so far removed from the normal associations that one tends to forget that the rules of logic should apply here as well as in towns and cities. I think that the acute fear that sometimes comes to a man in mountain places is due to the fact that he is alone with unknown things. Above and below him are mysteries: the sky, far and vast, and the thought of whose infinity makes the mind tremble; there are the winds, capricious and unseen; there are the streams whose waters have washed every shore and river-bed in the world; and mountains, cast up in unknown ages. And here too is a slab of rock which has fallen across two others. It has lain like this from before the dawn of life on earth. It has preceded man.

And in the midst of all this is the greatest and most terrible mystery of all—the presence of the striving non-Comprehender, a reasoning flash of consciousness that gives existence to all else, a Mind in the centre of inscrutable Matter. If one should reflect thus, would it be so intolerable to see a being peculiar in certain respects, transparent, perhaps, where we are opaque, larger than is considered usual, pursuing a course of life unlike to ours? Would we cry out and rub our eyes in doubt, saying, "It cannot be so!" when we ourselves are only drawn from the unknown by the unique courtesy of the Unknowable?

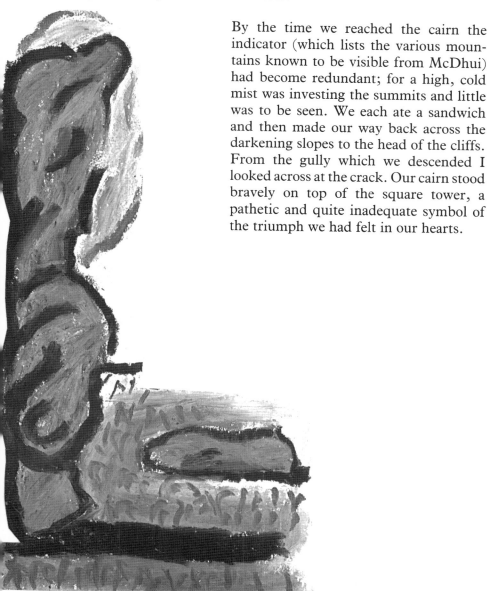

By the time we reached the cairn the indicator (which lists the various mountains known to be visible from McDhui) had become redundant; for a high, cold mist was investing the summits and little was to be seen. We each ate a sandwich and then made our way back across the darkening slopes to the head of the cliffs. From the gully which we descended I looked across at the crack. Our cairn stood bravely on top of the square tower, a pathetic and quite inadequate symbol of the triumph we had felt in our hearts.

hALCYON DayS

I t was as calm an evening as any since the beginning of the world. The whole island slept under a blanket of heat. In Glen Brittle Lodge my friends and I deposited our climbing gear, announced our arrival and went to our rooms. An hour later, we were seated round the supper table, eating as well as the heat would permit.

"It can't last," said the tall man, referring to the weather.

"I'm afraid not," answered the small man, wistfully.

When we had finished eating we went to the lounge where there were five or six other climbers all talking in low voices. The small man and I were engaged in a lively discussion when a young man rose haughtily to his feet and said with some distinctness: "This is supposed to be a reading room." Other men in the room looked up and gave us negative glances. We looked suitably unmoved, muttered some platitudes and slunk outside.

In the sheer wonder of that summer's evening we soon forgot the boorish one's remark. The mountains were lapped in warm mist: the sea was without a ripple and there was not a breath of wind. The moors which led up to the mountains were cracked and dry and exuded the scents of thyme and aromatic peaty heather. Walking through the Lodge garden with its profusion of undergrowth and heavy, silent trees, we slowly mounted the hillside towards the Eas Mor while from unseen places the cuckoo's voice charmed the evening with it's captivating monotony. Reaching the edge of the Eas Mor's gorge we saw a waterfall dying in the heat, its flow emaciated and spectral. We sat down on the warm earth, and looked around. The summits of the hills were bathed in a universal flush of pure, warm light and beneath us the Lodge lay within its tiny circle of trees, a thin line of smoke rising vertically from one of its chimneys. "It isn't often like that," the tall man said, and furrowed his brows as his mind went back over fifteen years in an effort to remember a time when it had been. "It can't last!" he said sadly, as we turned back towards the Lodge.

The next morning no one was keen to confirm the expected collapse of the weather, and as the small man drew the blinds aside and looked out he said nothing for a moment, but walked back to his bed, and still no word escaped him. Having seated himself on the edge of his bed he sighed deeply in great satisfaction. "Well?" asked the tall man and I in one breath. He smiled happily and said, "It's fine," and sought his shirt among the bed-clothes. The small man was a mountain lover and this was his first visit to Skye: so his reactions to what is normally a matter of small import were exaggerated. For months he had looked forward to these three days, and how vital it was then that the mountains of which he had dreamed should be visible on his first visit to them. That is why his face shone like the sun which was even now drawing its glory across the eastern waters of the Minch.

The tall man and I were dressed in a flash, washed briefly and then went downstairs and hovered around the dining room. We were rather early for breakfast and while my two friends wandered into what we now referred to as the "quiet" room I went outside.

I suppose it was like any other summer's morning in any other beautiful place, yet to me there was an additional element, in that I was in sympathy with the morning. I have forgotten what I was thinking then, but never shall I forget how beautiful the morning was, how the unseen cuckoo sang in distant glades, or what we did in these three days. Memory seems to take no note of the mental states contemporary with them, and so this joy is deduced from my present reactions rather than clearly associated with the *self* of then, yet there are these circumstances: it is summer, the self is free, with no demands upon his freedom; he is young and strong and about to climb the mountains that represent his greatest pleasure and, most importantly, he is devoid of all mental activity other than a spontaneous reaction to these circumstances. Everything else is forgotten.

Memory in recovering the events of those three days calls for a renewal of them on the grounds of their intrinsic excellence, but fails to register the then active regret that they were compressed into so short a space of time. There was most certainly the unconscious fear of possible death, and there must have been a multitude of other long worries or urgent problems, to cause a bane upon the absolute bliss in that adolescent mind. And so it is the activity that remains as the welcome guest in my mind long after the mental door closed upon its then accompanying traveller, thought.

"Whither is fled the visionary gleam?" asks Wordworth sadly, and has no ready answer.

The small man tapped my shoulder with the news that breakfast was ready.

"A show of hands is required," said the tall man jovially. The point in question was whether we should postpone our arrival at the rocks long enough to immerse ourselves in the crystal waters of the Faeries' Loch, and it was carried unanimously. We had not been walking for more than half an hour, but the sun had climbed high into the sky and the heat was becoming intense. We removed our few clothes and with a concerted rush made for the loch: three splashes, accompanied by shouts of joy, announced our entrances.

It was superb. The remarkably warm water was more like a tepid bath even where my limbs cut the brown depths, and I soon turned over on my back to float gently. The sun beat down upon my face, and filtered light upon my body. I could see the calm surface on a level with my eyes and the great mountains beyond it rising in a shimmer of heat. "Isn't this wonderful!" I shouted to the tall man, who was treading water nearby. We sported in this fashion for fully half an hour and would have delayed longer had not the rocks looked so inviting.

We did not bother to put on our few clothes but walked in a naked state until we had dried in the sun. By then we were entering the mouth of Coire Laggan and the enormous precipice of Sron na Ciche aroused our amazement. This mammoth wall, which rises sheer for nearly a quarter of a mile above the floor of the corrie, is seamed by deep gullies and ribbed by pinnacles. Almost in the centre of it is a fantastic knob of rock balanced at the top of a long slab. This is the Cioch, or breast. It was our intention to enter the gully which divides it from the main precipice and thus approach it from behind.

A small path, worn by the boots of thousands of climbers, led us to the base of the cliff and we walked slowly along it towards the gully we had selected. Every now and again we noticed a line of white scratches leading upwards by narrow cracks, or even over the faces of open slabs, and these marked the start of some route or other. They resembled ancient hieroglyphics, each of them standing as mute evidence for some deed of skill and daring. Before long we reached the mouth of our gully and seated ourselves on warm boulders to exchange our boots in favour of plimsolls.

For the most part we found the gully very easy. Near the top an enclosed chimney demanded a small expenditure of energy, but no angle of these warm, rough rocks seemed steep enough to daunt the adhesive capacity of our plimsols. Above the chimney we found ourselves at the end of a wide terrace which seemed to lead round the base of the Cioch itself. The rock rose above our heads like a great, mis-shapen, window-less barn. We walked slowly around it until we were presented with a long, smooth slab. This was steep and definite holds were few, but the texture of the rock was so rough that we found it quite easy; within ten minutes of starting to climb we stood on the summit of the Cioch.

Much has already been written about this place, and I will simply remark that on top of the Cioch I was aware of two very diverse sensations. One is aroused by a single glance at the gargantuan walls above my head from which the rock seems to sprout like a wart upon a giant's face, while the other is elicited by a brief survey of the equally vast shapes beneath. The first impression is one of immense solidity; pillars of stone seem to descend and grip the Cioch. It is like a gargoyle seen from above which depends more on the jutting battlements than on the walls supporting them both. Then one looks down and the illusion is no longer of strength but of too great weakness: gone is the sense of security, gone the idea of solid massiveness. Now one stands upon a flake of rock which maintains its uneasy position by the grudging permission of the gods of gravity.

Hundreds of feet beneath, mighty blocks lie in confusion upon the corrie's floor and bear ample witness to the mutability of the precipice. And great changes are always taking place; the edge of the Cioch is undercut by an overhang and in wild weather blasts of windy rain sigh eerily across its projecting shape, making as sad a music as one would expect to hear across the fatal waters of the river Styx! The Cioch is indeed a fit altar for this high temple of decay.

We lay in the sun on it's sloping roof. The small man was too amazed to say a great deal, and his conversation was little more than a series of "Oh's" and "Ah's." The tall man and I compared the prevailing conditions with very different ones two years before. Nowhere else in Scotland do weather conditions count for so much; in rain, Skye can become purgatorial, a place where anxious climbers languish in bouts of terrible impatience and get badly on each other's nerves. If they have time they sit about and read for days on end. If not, they go home. He who waits long enough (and, alas, how many have the necessary leisure?) will wake one morning and see the hills parting from the mists, and his heart will swell with happy anticipation of dry rocks and long views from clear summits.

Before we left the top of the Cioch for the eastern gully the tall man summed up our situation,

"This may be the last time I shall ever see weather like this here. It comes most often at this time of year, but I don't! I'm given a holiday of a few days annually—not at the same time—and the law of averages tells me

that I shall be very lucky indeed if the time of my holiday and the advent of fair weather overlap again." In view of this rather depressing fact, I resolved to make the most of my last two days in Paradise, and of this one which was already more than half spent.

We traversed into the gully by a narrow slit above the great slab. This is a fearsome place filled with enormous blocks of rock. About two hundred feet above the point where we had entered we found a ponderous mass of gabbro lying across our path like a fossilised (but none the less vigilant) watch-dog. This problem can be overcome in two ways: one consists of a long stretch and a strong pull up the small wall directly to the left of the stone. The other method demands far less energy: the stone, in falling into its present position, left a tiny gap betweeen itself and the gully wall. Most bodies, suitably manipulated, could probably pass through it if they had time. Here is the rub: the gully is often filled with water. At the stone the stream divides; and while some of it cascades over the wall, and thus materially increases that problem, a fair proportion finds its way through the gap. Kenneth, on a former occasion, had been driven into attempting a passage of this through route, (since neither of us could climb the wall). The holds on the top of the latter were inundated and our hands were too cold to grip anything for very long, so Kenneth decided to enter the breach. The first thing to alarm me after he had been gone for a few moments was the gradual diminution of the water from a sizeable stream to a tiny trickle. I began to have terrible visions of my friend becoming jammed in the opening and being rapidly drowned; just as I was about to catch hold of his legs in an attempt to free him, a great gush of water reassured me. His legs were quickly drawn up out of sight, and I knew that he was beyond the difficulty. My turn had now come. The rope was thrown down and I tied it round my waist; a single long stride took me on to a tiny, insecure foothold; my hands closed over a rounded edge. The main flow of water was rushing down the wall a few feet to my left and, just as I was about to pull myself up—aided by a strong pull from Kenneth—my hand and foot holds gave way and I swung into the stream! The next five minutes were passed in a strenuous struggle, in which the forces of gravity and weight of falling water on the one hand, and the strength of Kenneth and my own reduced efforts on the other, were almost equally matched. In the end we triumphed and I landed, gasping, at the top of the wall.

HALCYON DAYS

I was relating this story to the small man as we neared the place, but so ostensibly changed were the conditions that he failed to register the required alarm. Now we overcame the block by the methods most suited to our individual statures: the tall man extended a long arm to the top of the wall and drew himself up, and the short man vanished into the cleft. Not wishing to add an anti-climax to my tale, I avoided both ways and found a moderately difficult chimney further down the gully.

We were now above all problems and only steep scree remained between us and the plateau of Sron na Ciche. So far the towering walls of the gully had limited the view, but now a remarkable sight was presented to our eyes. The further island distances and the shores of the Scottish mainland were hidden by the heat haze, but their exclusion only added to the savage splendour of the jagged summits which reared up from the Cuillin ridge. In a dozen places the azure serenity of the sky was seared by these fantastic outlines. The eye, travelling along the ridges, had constantly to be lifted or depressed while the mind almost revolted against the idea of a country so torn and ragged. Far beyond the plateau on which we had emerged, Sgurr Alisdair rose in confident supremacy, not only by reason of its few extra feet, but because of the tapering kingly shape and the sanity—rare in these hills—of its graceful outline. Beneath us, to the right, was a rock-girt bowl, a scoop which might have been the work of a giant's trowel, in whose grey and slatey depths lay a tiny pond like a baby's blue, unwinking eye. Of the other islands only Rhum was visible, and it was so vague and pale that one could hardly believe in it.

We set out for Alisdair after a brief rest, and during the subsequent passage of the tortuous ridge we began to find the sun a little too intense. It blazed down upon us from a position almost directly overhead and, even at this height, there was hardly a breath of wind. The rocks, too, had grown very hot to the touch. We came to, and crossed the so-called "bad step" in the ridge to Alisdair without taking much note of it. Very shortly afterwards we were grouped round the cairn upon the highest of the Cuillins.

The day ended, if I remember correctly, in three very pleasant things. The first was a wild, exciting and dusty dash down the famous "stone chute" into the head of Corrie Laggan: the second, a drink at a small, ice-cool spring near the bottom of the "chute"; the third, another swim in the Faeries' Loch—a rare holiday for our tired feet. We spent the long evening by the open window in the "quiet room" while the cuckoo's note became ever clearer and sweeter and the setting sun gilded the last battlements with living fire.

The following morning there was less suspense about the state of the weather; but even so we drew the blinds hastily aside, as though the sun were a fawn that must be caught suddenly or lost forever. It was fine. Today we intended to visit Sligachan and climb on Sgurr nan Gillean and its associate crags. In addition, I had a little private plan that I was keen to put into operation. My idea was to force a passage through the cavernous Bhasteir gorge, swimming when necessary and climbing where possible. My two friends preferred the *terra firma* of the low ridge and looked upon my plan as a piece of madness, so when I left them and said goodbye, they wished me well with touching, but somewhat depressing sincerity. I felt that they had no real expectation of seeing me again!

I walked along the right bank of the gorge until the walls began to rear up around me. As soon as the stream became narrow and constricted I took the left hand wall, crossing by means of a series of small but adequate ledges and continued deeply into the gorge until the light began to change from the pure white of the summer's noon to a shadowy greenness. The ledges began to fail, and soon it became apparent that I should have to swim. I removed my clothes and put them in my rucksack. Within a few moments of doing so I came upon a sheet of water of formidable proportions. The rocky bowl containing the pool was oval in shape and its sides were inclined in smooth overhangs; it was quite obvious that there would be no footing beneath the surface of the water. At the pool's far end was a large jammed stone on either side of which a thin but persistent stream cascaded down. There was nothing else to do but swim and trust to luck that I could find a way up the wall beneath the stone. I must confess that the thought of entering that lonely pool filled me with vague misgivings. Then there was the rucksack to be considered: how was I to convey this across the pool without soaking my clothes? A spare rope I carried provided the answer, and with one end round my waist and the other securely tied to the rucksack, I lowered my body into deep water and began to swim towards the waterfall.

The temperature in these shadowy depths was very different from the tepid joys of the Faeries' Loch! There was a subterranean nip to this crystal element, with the curious feeling as though a vertical current of water were being pumped up directly beneath me. It was a little alarming and I was not sorry to feel the spray of the waterfall on my face. I trod water and examined the left hand wall: there were a few small indications, a narrow crack, a tiny knob of rock. They were all placed in awkward positions, but the right wall gave me still less encouragement. I began to think that this problem was insuperable when I noticed that behind the left cascade the rock was broken and fissured. Knowing that if I contemplated this place for too long I should abandon it, I immediately gripped an outstanding rock and pulled myself into the water-fall. The stream lashed my face and shoulders, but I persevered and presently it became possible to move to drier regions. A few feet from the top of the stone I suffered a set-back: the holds came to an end, but I was over-confident and, balancing on a slippery surface my left foot slipped. I caught desperately at air and fell backwards. For a moment my mind was centred on the chances of striking a submerged rock and being rendered unconscious; it seemed to take an age to descend less than twelve feet. Then the

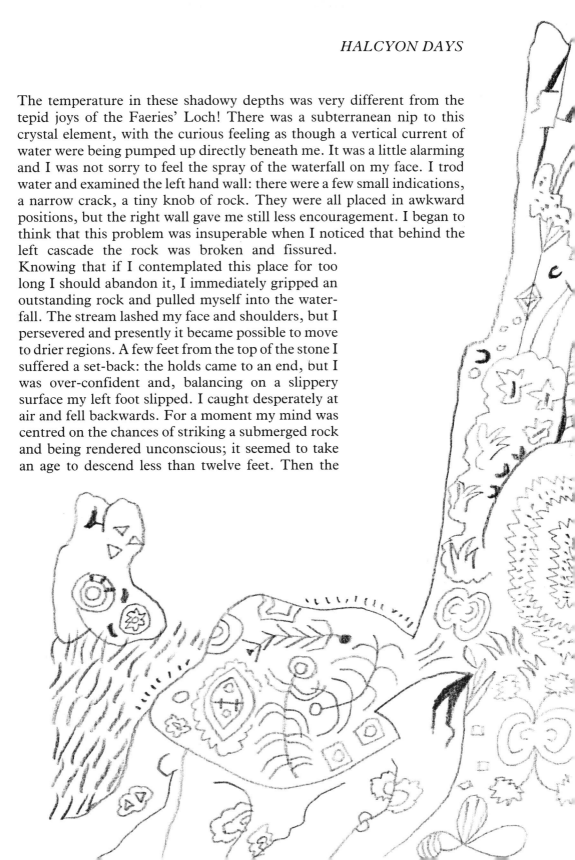

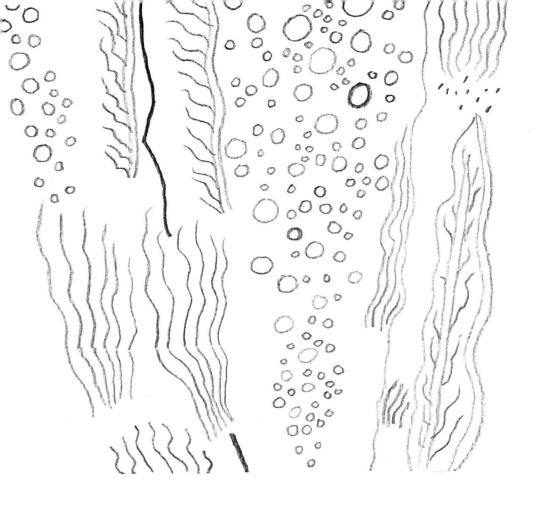

kindly, yielding water closed over me, cushioning my fall and bearing me gently into regions of green water, flecked with crystal bubbles. I lightly grazed my right foot on a rock as I kicked out to return to the surface, but no other damage was done.

So pleasant had been this brief experience that I would gladly have undertaken it again had not time required me to continue. So far, I had not taken very long to reach this point, but it was impossible to judge what barriers lay ahead and I did not want to delay my friends. I climbed back beneath the line of falling water and, with great care, managed to overcome the smooth final portion. The top of the stone formed a tiny island in the stream: I stood upon it and prepared to collect the rucksack.

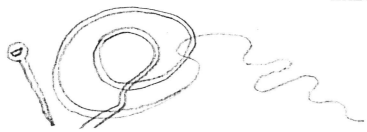

Snatching in the slack rope I gave a couple of long pulls. The rucksack rose as though a magician had laid a sudden spell upon it and swung straight into the waterfall where it hung long enough to ensure that all my clothes were inundated! I loudly uttered a remark which modesty forbids me to record, and turned to the next part of the climb. This was a smaller edition of what I had just climbed, but proved easier, however, and beyond it the terrain was similar to that at the entrance to the gorge. A brief period elapsed while I put on my drenched garments and quitted the gorge, the heat of the sun beat down on me again. I saw my friends seated at the bank of scree and great was their pleasure—and surprise—at finding me alive and well. They were as anxious to hear of my experiences as I was to relate them, and we decided upon the moment as an opportune one in which to dine. Sandwiches made their several exits from the depths of rucksacks— although I was only able to produce a sodden conglomeration of yeast mixed up with jam and cheese!

Our next undertaking was the ascent of the Basteir Tooth. We climbed slowly up the punishing scree to the ridge at the head of the corrie, and gave long gasps of relief as we found a tiny stream of cool air passing across it. From the crest of the ridge we stared up at the Tooth. It is unique in Scotland: there is nothing to compare with it. From here it arches above one's head like the blade of a scimitar, while from a little way down the scree it justifies its name and resembles a huge, cruel and decaying fang. The route we had chosen leads up the vertical rocks of the southern aspect. It is short and sensational, and has the peculiar attraction of being quite invariable. It is impossible to diverge by as much as a foot from the accepted line of ascent which is closely invested on either hand with stark overhangs and polished slabs. It seems as though the Architect who planned it had paused to consider posterity and had favoured mountaineers with special encouragement. We climbed the route slowly with connoisseurs' appreciation of the exposed situations and rough, sturdy rock.

At the summit, as airy a spot as one could wish to find, I left my two friends and descended to the corrie by a long and easy route. There was one climb on the Tooth still unknown to me: I had read that the ascent of a certain chimney led to a tunnel in its roof, and that from here a passage travelled upwards and inwards, and that by perservering in these secret places within the body of the Tooth one might find a tiny opening which would bring one back to the light of day upon its summit. The thought of this had fascinated me, and I had long since memorised the instructions for reaching the heart of this novel situation. First one follows a ledge along the face of the Tooth. I found this easily enough and then sought the overhang which was reputed to be above it. The passage of this proved to be a hard struggle, but, once over it, a sloping rocky floor led me to the base of the promised chimney. Here I employed the method known as back-and-knee and climbed steadily upwards on glorious holds until I banged my head on the roof. This was a queer spot! As far as I could see—for there wasn't a great deal of light—a tiny, dark passage ran upwards from the back of the chimney. Into this cavity I introduced my shoulders and was delighted to find that there was much more room than I

had imagined. My legs followed slowly and I was then forced to adopt a painful, crouching attitude upon the floor of a rocky passage. I worked my way forwards—very slowly and with some difficulty—and was beginning to feel a certain degree of panic in my restricted situation which a distorted mutter of voices somewhere above my head did nothing to dispel.

The passage came to an abrupt end. Would it be possible to go backwards? I wondered. I raised my head cautiously and shouted:

"Hullo! Can you hear me?"

Startled exclamations from immediately above my head confirmed my suspicions as to where I was. A layer of jammed stones, probably a thin layer at that, stood between me and a long drop: I had advanced too far over the chimney and passed the upward passage. Beginning to wonder if there was anything I could do, something tapped me on the leg. Cringing at the touch, I had visions of enormous rats! Then I heard the tall man shouting, "It's here. The hole's here!" After a strenuous wriggle—in which I compared my sensations to those of a baby being born—a patch of blue sky was suddenly revealed to me at the top of a narrow gap. A length of rope was dangling through this, and above it the face of the small man was visible. Both my friends regaled me with words of encouragement, and a titanic struggle followed in which I lost a good deal of red, sunburnt skin to the mountain. At length my head and shoulders were inserted in the vertical funnel. A further period of reduced exertion served to return me to the light of day.

When I had rested and recounted my story we climbed on to the Basteir—the Tooth's less exciting neighbour—and then descended the ridge in the direction of Sgurr nan Gillean. Whether to ascend this mountain was debated for some time: we finally rejected the proposal. The heat had tired us in the two days and a degree of apathy, unnoticed except in our lowered enthusiasm for further activity, had set in. We had been invited to dinner at the Sligachan Hotel and the small man, whose holiday had now come to an end, was not coming back to Glen Brittle with us.

HALCYON DAYS

The next morning the sun was still shining. We undertook a modest programme for we were now really affected by the heat. We forced ourselves a little and our idolatrous worship of the sun-god was over. We would have given quite a lot for a shower of cooling rain, and the cuckoo had several times been condemned for his persistence, especially late at night. I cannot remember very much about the third day, and will leave it in an oblivion from which it probably has good reason to settle. Those first two days were halcyon days... they ended before the heat exhausted our bodies and blunted our appetites for exertion.

As the tall man and I were driving back from Sligachan on the evening of the second day, where the Glen Brittle road is joined at the tiny school house, we stopped to enjoy the evening from that highest point.

My limbs were warm and tired and I was pleasantly conscious of having eaten a good meal. The scents of bog myrtle and thyme were heavy on the still air. The expanse of Carbost Bay lay at our feet, barred by the setting sun. Traces of distant islands were seen rising like half-formed thoughts in the azure and silver vastness of the sea. We had climbed for two days: there was one more to come, and in that thought the hinterland of Paradise forever gleams.

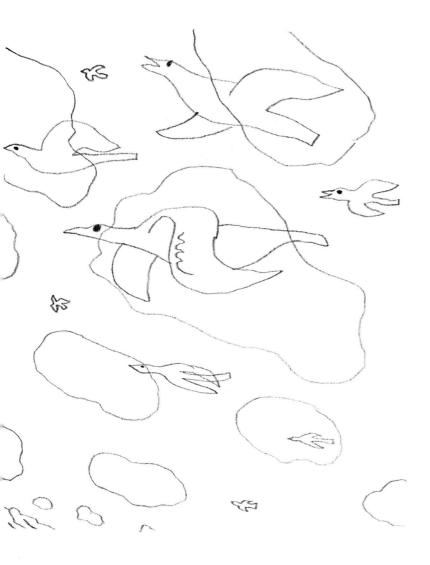

SONg
TO High NOON

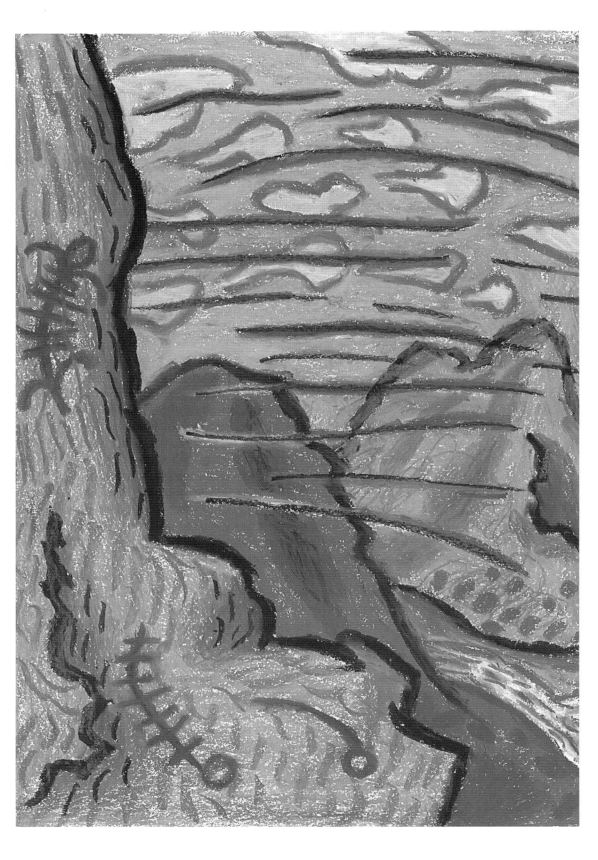

the Contest on the Heights

Iain and I met on Ben Nevis. The three of us (Kenneth made up the trio) enjoyed a week-end of strenuous climbing under wintry conditions. We did the climbs of the greatest severity on the first two days; on the third the weather had so degenerated that we were unable to undertake a rock climb and limited our ambitions to a snow gully.

We left the climber's hut and strode out confidently into a grey dawn, climbing slowly over the tumbled snow-covered boulders in the glen. The exertions of the last two days had been heavy and we had lost a great deal of natural heat; the clothes we wore had not dried since our first climb and the wind blew into them with the steady strength of early dawn. Once above the boulders we came upon a snow-field of agreeable firmness, and the next twenty minutes passed happily in cutting a staircase up it with axes.

Our first objective was the mouth of a deep gully that separates the projecting mass of the first platform from the main bulk of the buttress. When we were some three hundred feet beneath this point the wind dropped slightly and a steady sleet began to fall. Simultaneously a thick mist drove across the face of the mountain and the dark gully closed us in.

Such a scene defies accurate description, but above our heads, so steep that one's head had to be flung back in order to see it, hung the buttress—an immense shoulder of rock ribbed in a skeleton of ice. The wind was blowing the snow across the face to the east and from the sharp line of the ridge in that direction a great plumes of snow whirled away under dark clouds which continually changed their shapes.

The slope grew more precipitous. Soon we paused to take up our positions on the rope to a pre-arranged plan. Kenneth went first, myself in the middle and Iain (with the camera,) brought up the rear. We worked as a unit, Iain and I completing subordinating our ideas to those of our leader, for such discipline is essential on a difficult climb under bad conditions. We roped up smartly, held a short conference, and then our leader set to work. At this point the entrance to the gully was guarded by a wall of rock. This was not high, but steep, and the thick ice with which it was clad made it a formidable obstacle in our upward path. Kenneth, however, accepted its difficulties in silence and commenced swinging his ice-axe.

Ten minutes we waited. The click-click of the ice-axe soon became indistinct and his figure merged with the mist. The rope paid out slowly, foot by foot. Then it stopped and presently began to return. I had the unreasonable idea that I might have done better, and shouted up to him:

"What's wrong up there? Are you happy?"

"Happy!" roared the mountain echoes in response; but from Kenneth there was not a word. I called again, cupping my hands:

"What's wrong?"

Again the verbal boomerang came back and then, from an infinite distance it seemed, I heard his response:

"Yes, there is some trouble. Nothing much, and I am near the top" —and something else that only the mountain heard. The rope now ran out more quickly and then came three sharp tugs, an interval, and then another three. It was the signal to advance.

Kenneth had used his axe in a most artistic fashion. Each step in the ice wall was deeply cut and scraped out; for ten feet an artificial staircase led upwards, at the top of which the difficulty with which Kenneth had complained was apparent—a steep wall, imperfectly covered in snow, of a peculiar smoothness. To the left of this wall was a thick rib of dark ice and into this Kenneth's axe had made a deep incision. The notch was large enough to receive the toe of my climbing boot; I placed it in position and found it a precarious support. Our leader had called upon a high degree of climbing skill in overcoming this problem and his balance must have been superb. Placing my foot more firmly in the step I cautiously raised myself,

lost confidence in the movement, and started to retreat; my foot, at this crucial moment, trembled and the next thing I knew was the nauseating tug of the tightened rope around my waist as I swung across the ice-wall.

"Why are you hanging about?" joked Kenneth in very bad taste, "that hold I cut for you was big enough to put your knee in!"

"I didn't see it," I said defensively, "it was filled up with snow."

"Excuses, excuses—well, try again!"

This time, after a little consideration, I was successful. Iain enquired genially whether a mothers' meeting was in progress and "would we take him up?" He told us when he reached our stance that the part of the gully in which he had been stationed was peculiarly exposed to the snow, and one glance at his encrusted form convinced us that this was much less than the truth. The snow had found every crevice in his windproof jacket, though the manner of his recital, coupled with his bright smile, almost convinced us that it had been an enjoyable experience.

Now he demanded that we should pose for a photograph. We took up our positions meekly, like two frozen rocks stuck upright in the gully, and submitted to be immortalised.

The camera returned to its case, and we were climbing once more in weather that had gone from bad to worse. The snow now fell in huge flakes which came swirling in upon us from every direction. Sometimes our eyes were affected and we could not see what we were doing, while the gully rose above our heads in an endless array of snow and ice-clad rocks. The cold was intense, our clothes sodden and our movements were too slow to increase bodily temperature to any extent. Yet Iain's enthusiasm never forsook him and the ceaseless punishment of the wind, the increasing natural opposition of the climb, the endless gully, all these things seemed to stimulate him; and he climbed with an accuracy and purpose emitting such phrases as-

"What a wonderful place!" and "isn't that fine! "

The position of last man on a rope is not one of much satisfaction. He is the scapegoat for the leader and his second man, but Iain accepted this responsibility, and on his account we did not have a moment's anxiety.

As a leader, Iain climbed beyond the limits of security, but as a second man, he was superb. Whether his ability as a cragsman was the outcome of an intensely optimistic nature, or whether he was constantly unaware of the mountain's opposition was hard to distinguish. To watch him lead was a wonderful experience, touched with keen apprehension. There was always a rhythm in his movements and he never checked an upward spring.

Some two hundred feet from the top of the gully we held a council of war. For some time we had been climbing up a combination of snow and ice, and now the latter was beginning to predominate. The necessity of cutting steps in this solid medium reduced our progress to a snail's pace. Where a single swing of the axe had previously been sufficient to guarantee a deep and secure footing, now it had become essential to pause for a matter of minutes over a step. Time was passing and the prospect of being overtaken by night in this place was unthinkable.

To the north of the gully, steep but broken rocks led upward. To gain these it would be necessary to climb, or traverse, a vertical face of most forbidding aspect: but we had little or no alternative. Each of us in his heart considered the advisability of a retreat, but no one liked to mention it and, at this stage in the climb, it was problematical if this would have saved much time. Iain assured us that the back of the First Platform, a long slope of easily inclined grass, gave access to the floor of the corrie.

We essayed the wall. Chilled to the bone and blinded by the whirling snow, it was a grim experience. First Kenneth drew himself out of the gully while Iain and I, leaning on the shafts of our axes, gave him what moral support we could. Twice I thought he had come off the face, twice, by exerting all his skill, he confounded the apparently inevitable. Then I gave battle and Kenneth, at my request, pulled strongly all the time and I found little desperate difficulty. But, just below the top an event occurred that jeopardised our security to an alarming extent: I had thrust my ice-axe into my belt in order to use my hands freely. Suddenly it caught on a projecting rock, twisted head-downwards and slipped away into the abyss. Denied its essential services I immediately became a liability to the party, and our efficiency was reduced to an alarming degree.

We reached the top of the platform where the tempestuous blast assailed us with the ferocity of a wild animal. The snow drove by in a horizontal line. It was a fantastic place on such a day. Although almost sick with the cold, we were fascinated and had to remain for a little while. Then we began to consider the descent. Theoretically, since the wind had been driving in from the west, the back of the platform should have been almost free from snow; on this assumption we had based our hopes on a quick and trouble-free descent. But it was not so. The back of the platform, far from being a slope of easy, snow-clad grass and boulder, had become, by a trick of the climate, a sheet of ice broken only by projecting rocks and patches of hidden savage scree... a death trap of a most terrifying nature.

There were no alternatives. This descent had to be undertaken. It was unlikely that we could climb down the rocks into the gully by the route we had ascended: for a descent there would have been made into the teeth of the wind, and in our present state, it was doubtful if we could have survived this. To continue upwards to the summit of the mountain was out of the question; there was a thousand feet of rock above us.

We crept over the edge and started to climb down the slope. Every step had to be cut with accuracy. There was nothing I could do to help. I exercised extreme care and cursed the loss of my axe. My mind and my body were weary and desolate. Little things began to repeat in my head and the various tones of the wind sounded like human voices. I listened with a deep but detached interest: there was a whispering of childish notes that rose and fell; then followed the deep-throated growl of the tempestuous, snow-laden blast that died away in the thin whine of a beast in pain, and the sibilant hiss as the snow was whipped up in curling vortices. But, behind and beyond these natural sounds, there was the muttering of a mountain people and the hollow voices of elemental spirits. When cold and tired, or sick and frightened, one's consciousness is heightened and one becomes increasingly aware of these things that are embedded deeply in the foundations of fantasy.

Now the exertions of the last two days began to tell on us. We became acquainted with the breathless fear that is born of the knowledge that a vast process is going on with no reference to human affairs. We moved down slowly and the tremendous wind, veering east to west, ripped at us, tearing the snow from the slope. The very lids of our eyes were blown back so that they watered profusely and made the search for holds a blind groping upon a surface where nothing could be seen but snow.

I was afraid. It was not the fear of death that held me; one could easily conceive a blast of wind, even more tremendous than those before it, plucking us from our uncertain holds and dashing us down into the corrie. But the conception did not cease there for the great elemental drama that was going on around us caused the mind to falter and produce thoughts of death in terms of translation into one or other of the primal forces working upon the mountain: the voices in the wind now sounded very close and

clear. They raved and howled in ecstatic joy, the joy of motion and the joy of impact: and soon I was persuaded—and fear grew less—that it must be a grand thing to dash oneself again and again upon the mountainside, knowing no hurt, rushing up the gullies and streaming over the ridges and summits.

And so we came down falteringly in a world of ice-clad ridges, of mist and wind.

In these hours of the descent Iain's character was revealed to us, for there is no truer revelation of the inmost ways of someone's heart than during contact with the beauty or horror of a mountain. Kenneth and I saw him discard, as far as possible, his own safety, in order to give us the maximum aid. His position on this descent was that of leader: he moved last.

In the middle of the rope, it was I who relied directly upon his safeguard. Twice I misjudged holds (that an ice-axe might have cleared) and slid away towards the infernal chasm below. The rope dragged me to a standstill. The second time I went slithering over a small cliff, and the rope tugged me viciously before I had time to shout a warning.

Occasionally the mist drew back and revealed the corrie floor. It seemed a vast distance away from us and approached at a snail's pace, but at long last the angle seemed to ease slightly, and the smooth ice slope gave way to a rocky undulation that filled us with a wild optimism. It seemed as though we were near the corrie at last. We crossed the rock shelf and our hope gave way again to something akin to despair—beneath was a vertical drop.

Iain was convinced that we had approached the buttress again and that, by traversing to the south, we should come to easier ground. He told us of two isolated cliffs which he remembered having seen on an earlier occasion, and was certain that, if this was the top of one of them, we were no more than seventy feet from the corrie floor.

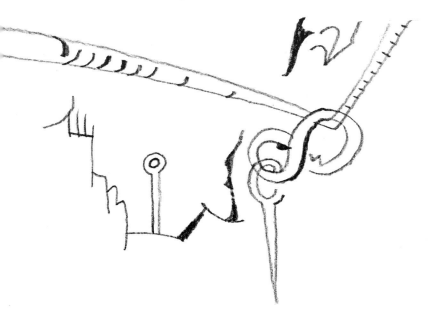

By now supposition had no power to cheer me, and I moved automatically between my two friends as they cut a horizontal path across the top of the cliff. It did not seem probable to me that we should ever find a way from the mountain. Suddenly Iain pointed down and shouted:

"Look!" Both Kenneth and I followed the direction of his finger, but all I could see was the tip of what appeared to be a precipitous sheet of snow. Iain had caught a glimpse of the corrie down this slope and it looked straightforward enough. Kenneth, without a word, drove the shaft of his axe into a drift and lowered himself over the brink. He kicked some deep steps, and then having removed his axe with difficulty, plunged it into deep snow some five feet lower down. Within fifteen minutes he was at the length of the rope, and I followed him over the edge. The angle was vertical—or slightly less—but Kenneth's steps made the descent an easy matter. Iain followed as soon as Kenneth and I were together, and on his arrival we repeated the manoeuvre. This brought us down by some fifty feet. Kenneth started out for the third time but before he had been gone more than a minute I felt the rope pulled sharply in while a voice, hoarse with excitement and relief, shouted up, "We're down!"

I communicated this welcome news to Iain, who took it calmly, and we both went over the final slope together. There was now no doubt that the climb was at an end; for the boulder-strewn floor of the corrie became visible before we reached Kenneth. The relief to us all was tremendous. Night, now no more than two hours distant, had been our most dangerous opponent, for I cannot think that anyone could have survived a winter's night on that open, ice-clad face. As I looked up at the swirling snow and heard the wind lashing the rocks it occurred to me that we had been unusually fortunate, and that, by the law of averages, we should not have returned intact.

We sat down and unroped, an operation which used up much valuable time, for the rope was hard and unyielding and our hands of little use. At length it was done and we strode away in the direction of the S.M.C. Hut. We would have been pleased to spend another night in it, but we felt that the ferocious weather would have been a cause of alarm to our relatives and that if we did not return to Fort William at once we might well be presumed dead.

Once in the Hut we made the inevitable cup of tea (the best, I think, that I have ever tasted) and packed the remainder of our clothes and equipment in our rucksacks. We tidied the Hut and then, for the second time within twenty-four hours, walked out into the twilight with feelings of regret, for it had been a good three days. We had not done everything we had set out to do, but we had enjoyed ourselves which is more important and assumed that rare spirit of companionship born in mutual adventure and which matures in times of danger. Three days before, Iain had been no more than an acquaintance: now he was a tried friend.

As we trudged down the rocky path beside the burn the mist was low and very thick but, as we left the shadow of the mountain, it did not seem to be so dark. Kenneth and Iain were ahead of me. Suddenly they both stopped and waited for me to come up—

"We were thinking of a holiday," said Iain.

"Good idea! I could do with one—where is it to be? On the Mediterranean, I hope. Warm sun for me from now on!"

"No. It's to be an Alpine holiday. We'll all go when the war's over and have a grand time. Come along now, and keep up with us! Let's make plans."

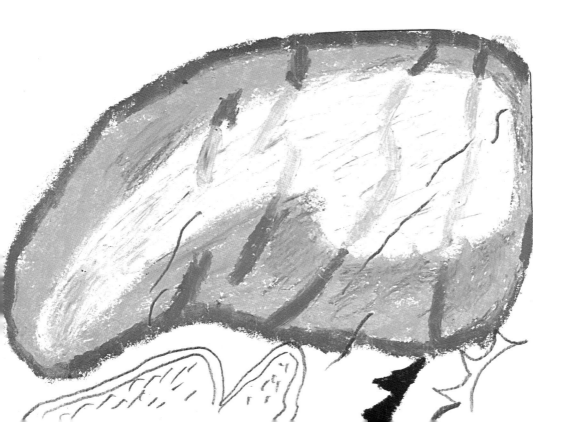

And many were the plans we made, and many the hopes we expressed that we would not have to wait long to put them into effect. On leaving the Hut it had occurred to Iain that such a successful team should meet again for greater undertakings on higher mountains. At first it had been a vague idea: yet before the bulk of Ben Nevis was lost in the mist it had become a reality. With laughter and gladness we spoke of the three days we had spent together: with keen enthusiasm we looked forward to many more. We made a happy trio as we strode down the path beside the swollen stream.

The darkness was low upon the ferny moorland and the mountain was more to be sensed than seen. Gravely its great bulk hung above the valley, guarding the little dwelling at its feet.

We paused to look back.

"Like a fortune teller, isn't he?" cried Iain, springing upon a rock, "he knows so much about us. The past, the present and the future are all one to him."

Kenneth and I smiled at these words that held a romantic appeal. But our friend had not finished.

"Yes!" he cried, cupping his hands, "Tell us where we shall be in a year from now: Oracle, answer me!"

Only the wind, running through the rain-drenched heather, answered him.

"Come now!" he continued, "and answer me, for if you won't tell us the future, tell us at least good-bye for the present!"

He stood, a lithe figure, his fine eyes fixed upon the mountain's vague shape.

"Good-bye, Ben Nevis, good-bye!"

We listened for the echoes' response. Flung from a rain-soaked rock in the misty twilight, running down the wings of the blast, came back the voice, but it was far and faint...

"Good-bye," and somewhere up there in the icy caverns the spirits that know all things added the one word—

"Forever!"

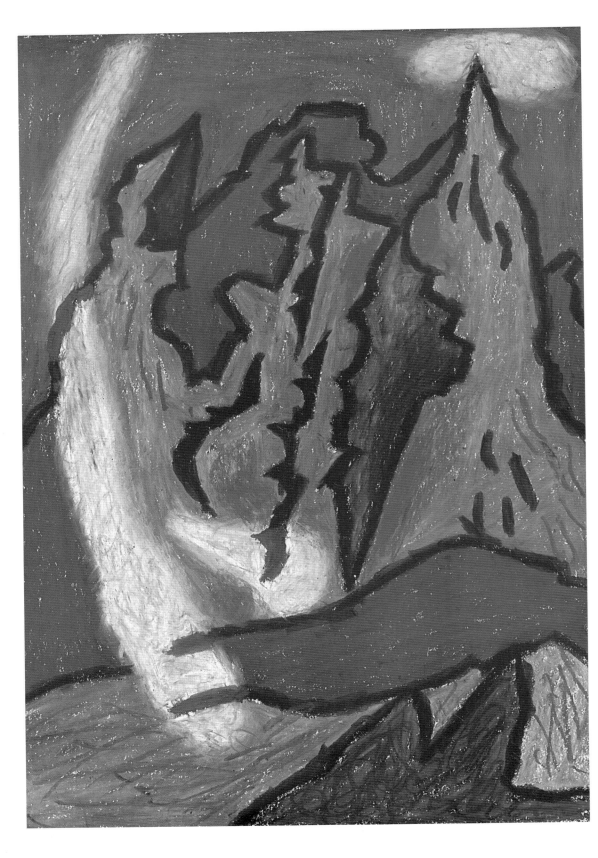

The Turn
of the Wheel

A few months later Iain and I met for a very ambitious attempt on a new climb in Glen Coe. We had corresponded frequently since the Ben Nevis venture and had done one or two minor climbs together. Iain, however, had been climbing regularly and, from news that I received of his undertakings, it seemed he was in splendid form. Nothing seemed to daunt him, and few crags to which he applied his unique skill denied him mastery.

We stayed at Kinghouse Inn, that remote habitation amid the long miles of Rannoch heather. Our first evening was spent studying the face of the mountain opposite—the stern Shepherd of Etive—which we had come to climb. The weather was set fair, dry and very warm. We went to bed that night in cheerful anticipation of an excellent day's sport on the morrow. After a dreamless sleep I awoke early to survey the weather. Signs and portents had not played false with us. The scaur of our mountain stood serenely up into an azure sky.

Our first day's climbing was in the Chasm: here Iain was not entirely happy while I was in rollicking form and took the lead. On this climb, in the heat of a glorious June day, I exhausted my store of nervous energy. Turning to each problem—and there are many—with a singular enthusiasm, I tried every trick of balance and judgement with which I was familiar. In doing so I stored up the products of fatigue in every muscle and was guilty of an extravagance in the use of energy that was to cost me dear the next day. In fact the first signs of exhaustion made themselves evident on the final section, known as the Devil's Cauldron for very apparent reasons, and produced feelings of panic in my breast. I climbed into the jaws of this fearsome object and was making reasonable progress upwards when a nameless fear gripped me and converted the healthy blood in my veins to the consistency of water. It is a notable fact that the hardest part of this climb is that which precedes its summit, but it was more than the natural hazards of the place that caused me to beat a hasty retreat. It had suddenly seemed to me as if someone had said,—"Look down! You will certainly be killed if you fall here "—and when I acquire a morbid interest in my position on a rock face I know from old experience that it is time for me to retire.

I offered the lead to Iain. For the first (and last) time while in my company he answered in the negative, declining to undertake the climb. He was certainly not his usual intrepid self; for I had seen him tackle obstacles far harder than this one appeared to be with great fervour and invariable success. This time, however, he was plainly convinced that he could not do justice to the problem and shook his head with a definite finality.

We left the gully by an easy 'escape' and reached the rocky crest of the 'Shepherd' just as the sun was gilding the mountains in their evening hues. Iain was plainly depressed. From my knowledge of him I realised that any variation from his usual form on a rock face was a matter of grave consideration to him. He spoke very little on the descent and return to Kinghouse.

As far as my own performance was concerned, it would please me if all record of the following day's climbing could be obliterated. For Iain, however, it represented a complete return to form, and he was suitably improved in spirits to sympathise with me in my pathetic efforts. We were a party of four on this occasion and it would have been better for all concerned if I had been far away. On one section of the climb I was incapable of a delicate manoeuvre and my failure to accomplish it led to a re-arrangement of the whole programme. The other members of the party used threats and persuasions in an effort to make me descend a ten foot wall. This place was abominably exposed; on its inadequate holds my fingers perspired in an agony of apprehension. All the time I was painfully *aware* of the immense exposure. I have always thought that it is the degree of this awareness that controls one's ability on a climb. If one can expel from one's mind all idea of the personal relationship to disaster the rest is easy and to me, on that awful day, the ghoulish spectre of mishap fell between me and every move I made.

I was placed last on the rope and it was a happy arrangement. There I could do the least damage. No sooner had I climbed the first pitch than I began to experience feelings of desperation and a prolonged wait in an uncomfortable position did nothing to increase my sense of security. The sun beat down on me unmercifully from a clear sky. I was out of sight from my companions and did not know what was happening. Now and again I could hear the rattle of falling stone and an occasional pointed remark. Once there came a mighty crash and an entire ledge was jettisoned into space. I followed its downward progress visually and saw it shatter into dust and fragments four hundred feet below. This, and sundry other alarms, did little to dispel my sense of impending disaster.

At last the three climbers had advanced sufficiently to take up secure positions and I was sent for. My attempts to leave my stance were appalling and had anyone been watching me they could not but have thought me affected by the sun. I fussed and fretted with the rope for an interminable period and then sallied forth on to the open face with my confidence at a low ebb. No sooner was I ten feet away from it than I wished myself back at my stance—which had the merit of a strong rock hitch for the rope—but pride compelled me to make some sort of a show.

The face of the cliff was very steep and cursed with an intrinsic rottenness that made every move a gamble with the laws of adhesion. Square-cut blocks of stone lay invitingly on shallow ledges, only to quake and wobble when tried with the foot. Handholds creaked and whole ledges of the larger variety drummed hollowly.

Iain, of course, was doing acrobatics in front. He was leading and doing it in excellent style: yet not for one moment could I conceal from myself that this whole proposition required me to take unnecessary risks. It was not justifiable in any sense of the word.

Soon I was ensconced in a tiny cleft, from where I could see exactly what was happening to my comrades and I found this comforting.

Iain had now reached the hardest section of the climb. He was performing miracles upon a vertical wall of rock, (the mere sight of which made me tremble.) This wall was part of a tilted fault that ran at a slight angle across the face. At one point or another it had to be crossed if the climb was to be completed. It appeared to me that Iain had deliberately singled out the steepest part of this barrier and was attacking it in a spirit of wild bravado.

He was no exhibitionist however, and I knew that his choice was prompted by some factor of which I was unaware and so intent did I become with watching his remarkable antics that, by leaning forward and undermining my centre of gravity, I all but fell out of my niche.

After what seemed like hours my friend had so far progressed as to get one arm and one leg over the top of the wall, and in a few moments he had disappeared beyond it. We all heaved long sighs of relief and shouted congratulations up to him. The position he now occupied was one of much greater security than any we had so far found on the climb. He was safely seated in a deep, incut hollow and, thus guarded from above, the two remaining members of the party made short work of the intervening stretch. When my turn came, I lumbered out of my niche, crossed fifty feet of decaying quartzite and approached the vital wall with defeat in my heart.

The situation was a dramatic one: far below me the screes of the gully stretched down to the moorland. So steep was the face that there was nothing to interrupt a sheer fall of some four hundred feet. The rock that composed the tilted wall was of a superior quality but abominably smooth.

With great caution, and testing each minute grip, I scaled the wall and joined my companions in the deep, incut hollow above it. Iain was wildly enthusiastic about the whole undertaking. So far the ground we had covered was virgin and beyond the hollow there was more to come. The hollow itself, however, was part of another climb we were crossing: the crux of this route was immediately beneath us and Iain, after examining the wall to our right, concluded that we must descend this.

Now, there exists in the minds of the uninformed a popular fallacy, to the effect that it is easier to climb than to descend a face of rock. In the usual state of affairs an experienced climber can always undertake the return with the same or lesser amount of difficulty. After all, a descent by a once-climbed route always constitutes a second journey—although one in reverse—and, in the nature of things, should prove easier than a first attempt.

But here it was not so. All the climbers in the party with the exception of my miserable self, had climbed this crux before. To me it was completely unknown. To descend it under these circumstances was for me a most hazardous affair. To add to my difficulties, since I was climbing last on the rope, this safeguard was now denied me. With a world of vacant space beneath I backed down, felt for holds, found none and withdrew to the top again. Words of advice intermixed with friendly abuse were flung at me, but it was to no avail. The place was too much for me. My honour as a climber was at stake, but it clashed with my safety as a human being.

So, due to my inability to descend this pitch, the traverse was abandoned for the day, and the climb we were on completed. Iain was determined not to end this holiday until he had completed the traverse. It was decided there and then to return and attempt it from the other end on the following day.

The next morning dawned fine again and we set out early in the direction of the previous day's climbing ground. A good night's rest had restored me to some show of enthusiasm and I had more animal energy, but only actual contact with the rocks would tell me whether my nerves had recovered.

By the time I had climbed the first steep rocks which led to the commencement of our route I was convinced that my form had improved. Iain and I were now alone; for our friends' holiday was over and they had left for Glasgow in the morning. We quickly reached the point from which the traverse was to start and rested here for a little while. In contrast to my feelings of oppression on the former attempt I was now full of enthusiasm for the venture and could hardly wait for Iain to lead away.

I was seated in a shallow declivity with the free end of rope lashed to an outstanding rock. My position was a firm one and the ground which Iain was covering was not difficult. I looked around me in pleasant appreciation of the scene. The great moor of Rannoch lay in front, surely the most desolate place in all Scotland. Its dark surface was broken now and again by a little eye of blinking light, a lochan bounded by peat. The clustered summits of Glencoe stole my eye as I looked to the east, but by far the most extraordinary feature of the landscape, however, was the immense rock face of the mountain on which we were climbing. Enormous pillars of weird natural sculpturing rose in titanic slabs, riven by savage gullies, and in the midst of such overpowering mass our physical insignificance was very apparent.

Iain had now reached a point some thirty feet away from me and shouted, "Come on now. There's a small stance here and some tricky work ahead."

I went over to him. He was balanced on the edge of a tiny sloping platform to which adhered a large, pinnacle-shaped boulder. My first words to Iain expressed doubt as to the adequacy of this stance; if he happened to come off the most I could hope to do was to hold him. There was little possibility of my getting enough purchase to draw him up again and he would have to climb the rope—an impossible task if he were injured in the fall.

Iain was worried when I told him my fears. He did not think that there was another stance in the vicinity: it would not have been practicable for me to hold him from our former position.

"Do you think it's justifiable then?" I asked. For a moment Iain did not answer. He carefully surveyed the remainder of the climb. From this position we could clearly see the point where we had given up the traverse on the previous day. Between it and us there was a smooth bulge of rock the far side of which was hidden.

"Not much use you going back to the other stance," he commented, "the rope wouldn't be long enough."

"No," I agreed, "but I don't fancy waiting here either."

He nodded his head in agreement. Then he put it to me quite frankly: Would I care to take the risk? Not much liking the prospect, I could hardly refuse after my own recent performance.

"Right!" I said, "go ahead and good luck to you!"

A moment later he set off round the last section of the traverse. Filled with doubts and apprehensions I watched him go.

My attitude in the groove may be described briefly. I was seated with my back to the mountain upon a ledge sloping outwards at an angle of about twenty degrees from the horizontal. This ledge formed the bottom of a shallow scoop, and the walls of rough but unbroken rock provided friction grips for both my feet. Behind me and immediately above my right shoulder was a large block of rock which was divided from the back of the scoop by a square-cut notch or neck. Over this notch and descending on both sides of the block the rope had been firmly secured.

Directly beneath the lowest extremity of the ledge there was a vertical section of rock which extended to a depth of some twenty feet; thereafter a series of impending overhangs actually undercut the ledge, my stance and my precariously balanced body. The situation was unnerving, to say the least.

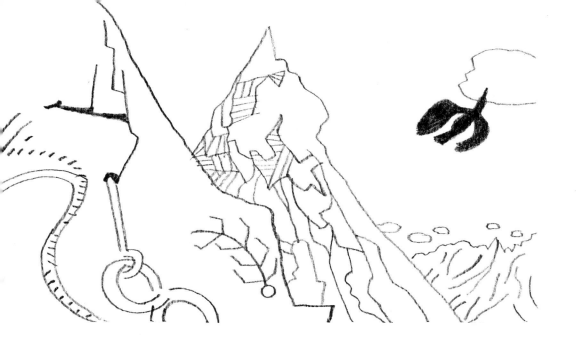

Iain was making slow but steady progress. Now and again he shouted to me details of the traverse, and I gathered from him that while the hand and footholds were minute, they were just adequate and quite firm. He was now no more than a score of feet from the comfortable hollow where we had foregathered on the previous day. This section, however, was not in my line of vision.

I had a sudden feeling of renewed apprehension at the thought of his disappearance round the bulge. While he remained in sight—and with a fairly short length of rope—I should have a small chance of averting total disaster in the event of his falling. Once out of sight however, there was very little I could do. Slight comfort was contained in the knowledge that he would approach the hollow from above and a fall in the last ten feet might not be serious.

Now he had reached the edge of the bulge. He seemed to find the climbing there much harder and for a minute he made no move. He volunteered no information and I dared not distract his attention by inquiring. Just at that moment I had the most terrible shock!

The better to see Iain's operations on the bulge I had leaned slightly forward and in doing so had brought to full stretch the rope that bound me to the block. *There was a sudden, harsh grating sound, and I felt the slightest pressure against my back.* I stifled an inclination to cry out. Without putting any tension on the rope I moved a little away from the block. There was no sound, and I breathed a sigh of relief. For a moment I had thought it was actually pushing me out of the groove. As often happens in moments of extreme desperation, I was vouchsafed a flash of cynical amusement. So this had been our sheet-anchor! Very cautiously I loosed the rope from the neck of the rock and settled down once again in my old position.

Iain was out of sight. There was not a sound and no movement of the rope. Sweat was running down my face. If only he could complete the traverse we would laugh about this later. But one false move on his part, one faltering step...

My attention began to wander. There was nothing more I could do for my friend or myself and, in the macabre possibility of the mishap, my time for other thoughts was strictly limited. I began to wonder what my parents and friends were doing at this very moment and how they would take the sad news—and at this thought I began to abuse Iain and myself for two inconsiderate fools. Why, in heaven's name, did we take that ridiculous decision when common sense should have told us that we were courting disaster? At this very moment, I thought, there are men giving their lives for their country and here are we jeopardising our own for the satisfaction of a mad whim! "God!" I said aloud, "if ever we get out of this scrape alive I am going to play safe in the future"—and at that moment *the block moved again.* This time there was no doubt of its lethal intentions for it was actually pressing against my back. I do not want to give the impression that I was holding the block in position against its entire weight, for it was resting on a slope of twenty degrees from the horizontal and required little to keep it in place. The moral effect, however, of this subsidence was terrible. I gave up hope on the instant.

The rope was paying out at a lively pace, but by then my pessimism was beyond alleviation. That block was threatening my life! It seemed that nothing could increase my fear when I glanced down and saw that the mountain had provided a shroud for us. An early afternoon heat mist had formed round its roots and the great dark cliff was swimming on a white sea. The effect upon me was both fascinating and horrifying. I was frozen

to the rock in a mood of cold panic, when I heard a shout of triumph:

"I'm over. I've a good stance here, so come on when you're ready."

It took me a little time to recover myself and bring myself back to life, so to speak. When I had done so my mood was aggresive. I shouted down into the mist with cupped hands:

"Way below there! Is anyone there? Loose boulder coming down! Watch out!"

No answer came from below but I heard Iain's bewildered voice inquiring what was going down.

"Our rock-belay!" I replied, and heard his astonished gasp.

I found a deep cleft for my fingers and swung my body clear. The block moved haltingly, jarred on the edge of the groove, slowly and deliberately turned over in the air and disappeared into the mist. A few moments elapsed and then came the echoes of the most tremendous impact far below.

"There, but for the Grace of God, went R. B. Frere!" I murmured, and moved away from the groove. The next twenty feet were hard, but I was still in a daze and did not fully appreciate the problem. Only after I had gone round the bulge did I realize how my friend's skill had won the day against incredible odds. It was twelve feet of traversing that defied the laws of adhesion and gravitation, that demanded absolute steadiness and perfect judgement. Iain's stance was some twenty feet higher up the commodious hollow. Halfway across the wall I told him that I was coming off, and a moment later swung gently into the gully.

Then I went up to him and told him that we had been fools to attempt it.

"Yes," he answered, "I know. But you see, I didn't know that damned spike was loose. I had decided to come back if, at any time, the traverse became too dangerous. But honestly, I felt in grand form and I don't think that there was much chance of my coming off. I'm awfully sorry about that spike though—I ought to have tried it."

There was not a touch of bravado in these words, and what should have been a boast in a lesser man was simply a statement of fact.

The climb was nearly over. The other half of the traverse, already vanquished, was avoided and we continued upwards by the same route we

had previously employed. It was a soft evening with mist cradling the
higher summits, and we paused for an hour on the crest of the
"Shepherd". The outlook was a broad one, with mountains predominat-
ing. It was very pleasant to lie against the cairn and rest tired bodies and
strained nerves. The air was warm on our faces as we retailed the accounts
of the climb.

"When's our next effort?" I asked.

"We could do something on Sgoran if you liked," Iain answered,
"there's a lot of new stuff there still. In fact, that reminds me of
something. Do you know the steep face to the left of the gully on the first
buttress?"

I knew it well enough. It was opposite that place that Norman and I had
climbed on the day of the thunderstorm the previous year. Unconsciously,
I used Norman's words:

"That's a treacherous place!"

"Isn't it? But I think it would go on a fine day in plimsols. See if you can
manage to come soon..."

I promised that I would come, but I did not climb with him again. The wheel of chance had turned full circle. Twice, minor things had caused me to cancel climbs with him. Then, for the third projected meeting, he was coming to visit me. The hour of his expected arrival came and passed into oblivion. It was not until thirty-six more hours had gone by that I learnt that Iain, having failed in his last contest on the heights, lay dead on Sgoran with a woman companion. That treacherous place, where I had promised to be with him, had proved too much.

After a momentary shock I entered a period of profound misery.

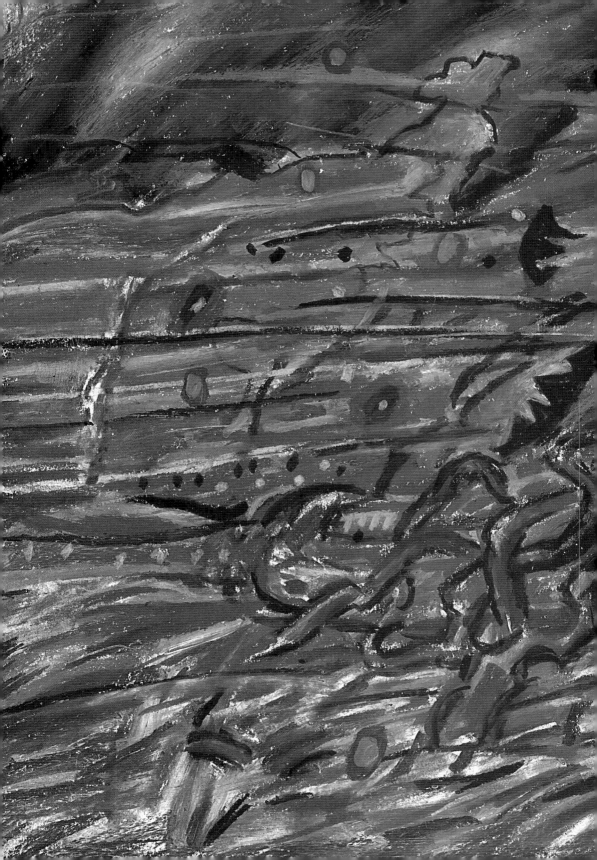

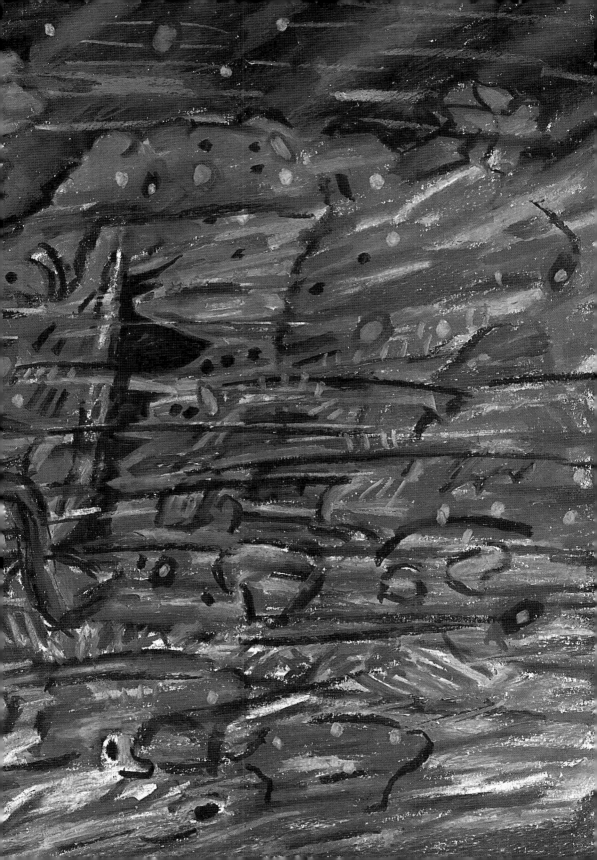

alone
in Solitude

It was a sad March day. The snow, a dirty yellow, lay on the hillside like a lingering guest whose welcome has expired. A harsh wind provoked one to movement, yet a heavy greyness in the air dissuaded it. A sprig of tender grass spelt hope, while a rattling burst of hail shouted despair. The elements and natural signs being thus at variance, the mind of man was agitated by doubts and assailed by fears.

The sky was packed with layers of clouds which resembled shadows through frosted glass, shapeless but with a regularity in their shapelessness. Where the sun stood there was a grey glare.

The ground had been whipped dry by the harsh wind, and its arid surface contrasted sharply with the little puddles of water that lay at the edges of the shrinking snow. Now and again a ragged bird sprang up and wheeled away upon the hollow sounding air; trees spread out their branches in amorous hope of the Spring which did not come, and the mocking wind moaned in their barren twigs.

Had I solicited the gods of nature to bring me a day to suit my mood they could scarcely have provided one more apt. There is sadness, too, in long slopes; the hill around me swept smoothly upwards. To me there is hope in steep contours, joy in sharp descents a sense of exaltation in narrow ridges: but in long slopes, I can find desolation and sorrow.

And so I walked on without persuasion from natural things. A resolve to reach the summit of this hill had actuated me, but it was the outcome of cold consideration and not of an emotional urge. As a man quickly returns to a sport at which he has been hurt or frightened in order to restore his nerve, so I came here to ward off a permanent aversion. The old urge was paralysed and painfully so.

My friend had been dead for six months. In that time I had undergone a comprehensional crisis, for whenever that scene on the Shepherd came to my mind I lived again the moment of amazement at his skill when I had joined him beyond the rock bulge. But then came a sudden devastation of the conception of safety that had been built up in me through years of apparent immunity to mishap.

Death, I began to think, had been our stealthy companion all the time, a dark shadow on the rock face with hands ready to punish the violator of natural laws. When climbing with Iain I had often doubted his analytical survey of its problems, but he had always served to convince me that there had been little danger. So now in retrospect, it no longer seemed to me that it had been his skill which had won the day: it was simply that the mountains had been very tolerant with him. And thereupon I ascribe to the mountains, a Will.

A few weeks passed and the initial shock faded. Essentially we had been climbing friends, for we had seldom met in any but the high places and, gauged by time our friendship had been a short one. Duration, however, was not a matter of importance, for in the mountains it is a notable fact that friendships mature very quickly, and the qualities that bring a man to the heights readily endear him to his friends. We had been through storm and tempest together; we had clung to the mountain wall and looked at the finality below; we had smelt the good scent of the heather and seen the sun set amid the valleys.

And so, although we did not meet more than a score of times, the passage of years could not have strengthened our friendship further.

Thus it might seem that by avoiding the hills—if only until Time's balm had worked upon the wound—I could have avoided the misery of memory; but for years the high places had exercised an absolute influence on my thoughts, and had moulded in me a philosophy of their own. To gain freedom from pain it was necessary to be free from thought. In thinking of books, of music, of anything other than the mountains, Iain did not exist: but to exclude hill-thoughts from my mind for any length of time was a thing of which I was incapable, and as soon as they returned he was there with them.

It was for myself, however, that I came to this hill. In the first days after the tragedy there was little pleasure in mountain thoughts, yet gradually matters improved as the mental ban imposed by the sudden shock relaxed. This was followed by the inevitable aftermath—a fearful apathy, which came at the beginning of the new year and lasted until March. It was during this month, with Spring hovering in the background, that I forced myself to undertake a climb; in order to readjust my conception of life and death and make my peace with the mountains, and to ascertain if the old appeal had lost its former strength.

The hill to which I went was an old friend, but could hardly be called a friendly hill. It was a titanic mound of reddish granite, almost devoid of the solace of trees around its flanks. Heather grew lank on its lower slopes; in the upper reaches a little moss clung tenaciously; its summit was a mass of ancient rocks, set chaotically in heaps, with here and there a dilapidated cliff overhanging a dark corrie. Decay ruled this mountain utterly.

It was a harsh choice, yet this one mountain could not be flattered by crying out to its beauty, for here all thoughts came inwards. Up the rough path I went then and, as I settled down to a steady pace, I began to reason.

My friend had loved the mountains. He had incorporated them into his soul, and the idea of them had become a part of his thinking being. His character had been built up to a large extent through contact with their beauty and terror, for he had approached them in a spirit of conquest, softened by adoration and a profound respect.

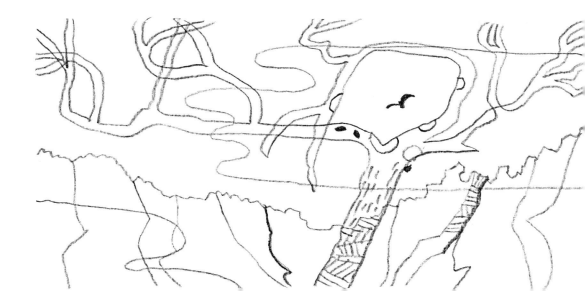

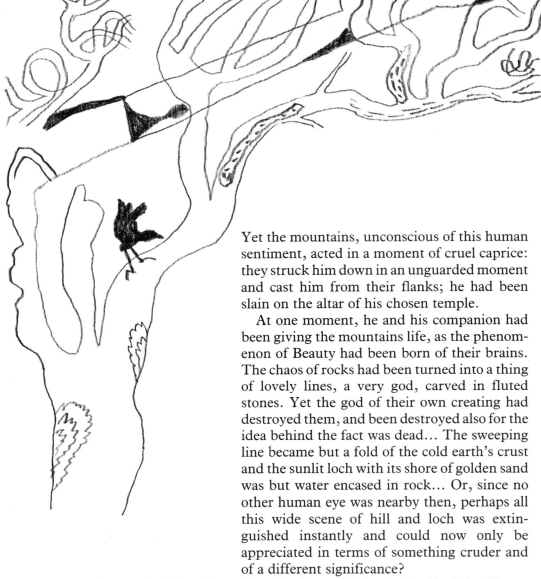

Yet the mountains, unconscious of this human sentiment, acted in a moment of cruel caprice: they struck him down in an unguarded moment and cast him from their flanks; he had been slain on the altar of his chosen temple.

At one moment, he and his companion had been giving the mountains life, as the phenomenon of Beauty had been born of their brains. The chaos of rocks had been turned into a thing of lovely lines, a very god, carved in fluted stones. Yet the god of their own creating had destroyed them, and been destroyed also for the idea behind the fact was dead... The sweeping line became but a fold of the cold earth's crust and the sunlit loch with its shore of golden sand was but water encased in rock... Or, since no other human eye was nearby then, perhaps all this wide scene of hill and loch was extinguished instantly and could now only be appreciated in terms of something cruder and of a different significance?

In my mind I could see the split ridge with the fatal gully, lying like an old wound between the wrinkled skin of the adjacent precipies. For I knew where they had been—moving upwards slowly—but how came it about?

There were a hundred chances, each potentially fatal. Alone in solitude, on this cold, dark hill, I could not bear to pursue the image to its dread conclusion and so again, in great bitterness of spirit, I uttered the old-age question, "Why?"

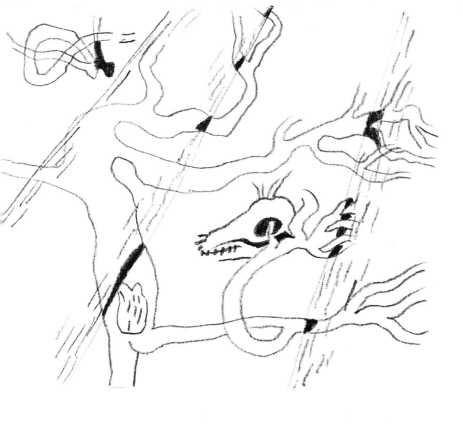

No answer came to my solitary voice, no response in the winds nor enlightenment fom the grey sky. The heather at my feet stirred and was still; a ray of sunshine struck the flank of a distant hill. Although I gave it life in my mind, the grey world stretched beneath my feet seemed locked in the unending stillness of extinction. Before me, across a mile of scrambled rocks, rose the summit of the hill. It was near; a half hour's climbing would bring me to it, but the old elation, even the sense of satisfaction that the thing was done, was absent. I sat down on a boulder, and with elbows on knees and head in hands, closed my eyes and tried to concentrate my thought.

Cut off from the world by closed lids, my consciousness bit in upon itself. Built of recollected experience, and harassed by that which had escaped from it, my memory strove to comprehend, but failed to understand itself or its singular function. Unalarmed by the darkness from which it emerged, it shivered in anticipation of the gloom which might well be its own end! A few minutes of consideration along these lines produced an elemental panic in me, and I arose to disperse my thoughts.

The grey of the sun was intensified, there was a subtle promise of warmth in the wind. A soul given over to melancholy will grasp at a little thing in order to dispel its misery, and a little thing is often capable of doing much to restore a happier state. The promise of fair weather did this for me. Within a few moments of rising from the boulder a sense of approaching optimism began, and my steps, as I tackled the slope, were quicker and filled with purpose.

There was no doubt that a change in the weather was at hand. The wind swerved from its pitiless eastern approach to bear with it some draughts from the kindly south. Overhead, compressed and clotted cloud racks were stirring uneasily and the white rose of the sun seemed about to burst from the sky.

The short heather brushed my feet as I walked on, but grew less as the altitude increased and soon gave way to barren and unfriendly masses of granite. Mighty slabs lay in chaos around; they resembled the scattered foundations of some enormous temple that had lain destroyed since the beginning of despair. Here and there a crystal slab of quartz glittered in its background of dull red. The rough terrain compelled swift and agile movement: it was not long before the summit was close.

From the rounded dome of the mountain, at high altitude, a great expanse of valley and hill was visible. Beneath me, a few hundred feet away, the swell of the hill was broken abruptly and the earth cleft by a deep rift. This cauldron fell away from the highest point of the hill in a steep slope of weathered granite and loose shale. Two ridges, joining at the summit, formed its sides. These sides were utterly diverse in character; for while that on the east was smooth, its companion to the west was broken into precipitous drops and vertical ridges, between which dark gullies wound their way into the very entrails of the mountain.

Behind and beyond this chasm the constricted valleys opened out into a wide plain, a green expanse of great pastoral beauty, upon whose surface dark patches indicated the presence of villages.

In the far west the promise of sunshine was fulfilled. The packed grey clouds were here attentuated in a long, thin line, beyond which the sky was blue. This sight awoke in me a feeling of happiness and a desire to reach the summit. I quickened my pace and, within a few minutes was seated behind the cairn.

With the exception of the profound declivity, the mountain was one of undulating slopes. To the north there was a great plateau of almost uniform height, barren as a desert. Here and there a fold of rock formed a summit and the general effect therefore, was not of height and depth, but rather of a devastated land, utterly lacking in vegetation, which could have been set at any altitude, in any land.

The heavy clouds still hung overhead and their compressed levelness brought a feeling of enclosure. It was as though the whole visible world was bounded by two horizontal lines. To disperse the faint uneasiness produced by this curious effect I walked slowly round the cairn and seated myself on its other side. Here the great cleft was visible.

This was a scene that no one, even the least impressionable, could regard unmoved. The world that lay at my feet had been twisted, shattered, beaten into shape, and torn and tortured into chaos. It was a world of lines that approached one another from all angles: pinnacles were flourished on high, great fragments lay in deep places. Their granite edges formed a million shapes and none of these could in any way be related to any other. It was a world of colours, though all were dark and sombre. In looking into these ancient depths and blue shadows that lurked between the bases of these twisted columns, where the wide field of broken rocks covered the floor, I was overcome by a sense of curious anticipation.

It was at this moment that my thoughts became centred again on my friend. It occurred to me how he would have spent these moments of physical rest in working out, in theory, some climb upon these cliffs. And, at this conjecture, emotion came strongly to me, I rose to my feet and said in an ordinary voice to the cleft's rugged wall:

"Whose idea was it that he should die at that moment?"

The words had hardly left my mouth when my glance became fixed upon the red cliffs. A quivering sense of anticipation held me enthralled and my whole body became tense.

Quite suddenly the outer wall of one of the buttresses seemed to move. It faltered. Then, from beneath it, rocks moved and rolled. The whole face of the buttress dropped, fell vertically, billowed out like smoke, and crashed into the depths of the corrie. For a moment not a sound came to my ears: it was more than a mile away. Then came a distant turmoil of sound. Rather, it was a combination of sounds and most prominent among them was a deep, savage creaking; this mellowed to a roar, with now and then a sharp report as individual rocks exploded in the general melee. Some time elapsed yet the roar went on. A great cloud of dust was sweeping up from the corrie and rose vertically until the wind, blowing over the ridge, caught it and carried it away.

The scene cleared a little, and I saw that the rocks were still bounding down the hillside beneath the crag. Great gashes were visible in the earth on this slope. The crag itself was horribly fissured, and the wall behind the collapsed section was livid like a scar. The echoes were ringing far and wide among the hills.

It was my answer. No more final response could I have invoked from the blind power that had destroyed my friend. The misanthrope in Poe's poem, confronted by the monosyllabic bird of prophetic ill, could not have felt more strongly the sense of tragic repletion that came to me then. Blind chance had done its work. It had fashioned the buttress in ancient days, it had dictated the hour, the minute, the second: it had decayed and worn away that which had been strong: it had caused the place, the fall, and the death: far in the hinterland of time had the roots of the tragedy been planted, and now the work was over and who could bear the responsibility? No thinking thing, no feeling, comprehending Mind, had done this act, no benign hand with dreams of design. No, only the forces that lift the wind without sentiment or guilt, the unindictable blind chance. Every day, every hour, upon the battlefield, brave, honest, joyous men were being rocketed to eternity upon wings of fire and steel. What dictated that this one should live, that one die? The same blind chance!

Hope drained from me and even the spring, blowing up from the salty coves of the western sea, could not elate my spirit now. Down in the corrie the dust was still rising, though now it was thin and like a haze of mist, yet still the deep echoes boomed in the recesses of the distant hills. But, as my thoughts entered the corridors of despair, I turned with bent head from the cairn and, without a backward glance, started to descend the mountain. The sun came out soon after and the sky rapidly cleared. Gone was the cold wind of the morning, gone the grey-packed sky. Life that had been suspended in the greyness now began again. Hares sprang up and loped away into the obscurity of the deeper heather. Even the harsh lichen on the ancient rocks seemed sympathetic to this mood of holiday, and the twisted roots of the vanished forests were like limbs that longed to stretch themselves.

I could not enter into the mood. I had seen what I believed to be a confirmation of a desolate finality. The spring would come again and again until the end of the world, and I had thought that we too would return, but now a thousand doubts assailed me. Not for a moment did it occur to me that my friend, whose character had been made supreme by the mountains, had now been united with them in a way that he never could in life—united, not with the image of beauty that depended on men's eyes and brains, but with the essential honesty of the elements themselves.

I passed through the few trees around the mountains flank and sensed that they too had found satiation of longing in the Spring, for there was a warmth of beauty here. A grouse cried across the moors. A few birds began to sing away the evening hours. Hurriedly I strode through the trees and down towards the lower inhabited lands, but my thoughts, like wolves, pursued me.

In this frame of mind I remained for many months.

gHoSts OFtHE pAST

Two years went by. Time, the great Obliterator—falsely named the Healer—had all but cured the wound that Iain's death had made in my adolescent spirit. The sharp pain was softened into the mellower sadness of memory; the horror that had once bulked large was now shrunk to an emaciated spectre. Yet still they lingered, this pain and horror, and especially so where the power of association was strong. There was not a day spent on the hills when I was not reminded of my friend and his untimely and tragic end.

It was again September when I approached Sgoran Dubh. We had come over Cairn Toul after two nights and a day of very ill-executed excursion. True, we had snatched this chance—Kenneth, Jimmy and I—from the jaws of the services. Kenneth's leave and mine had over-lapped. Jimmy was departing for the south in a few days. It was a last minute thing, a scramble of rope finding, rucksack finding and scraping up of food. And, two days earlier, when the light had been fading in a lovely September sunset, we had set out on foot, heavily loaded, to reach Aviemore by any means that presented themselves, which we did in the small hours of the following day and so set out again at once, sleeping in the dews on the pine-forest's floor when we were too tired to continue any further.

When we awoke, stiff and little refreshed, the stars were fading in the sky, and we climbed very slowly to the summit of the Lairig, pausing every now and again to sleep or drowse in the heather. Here Kenneth, his time having expired, left us and I thought, as I watched his well-known figure receding down the great roofless vault of the Pass, that perhaps we should not meet again: and I cursed the fate that had flung a War across our lives.

Jimmy and I continued to the Corrour Bothy, that tiny habitation set beneath the savage Devil's Point, where we lay down and slept away a night of cold discomfort and disturbing thoughts. At first light we made breakfast and, bowing beneath our packs, essayed the long, steep slopes of Cairn Toul.

It took us all day to climb that mountain, usually the work of a few hours. The weather held during the morning, but in the afternoon mist began to rise from the corries and the sky became overcast which persuaded us to attempt a short cut down into Glen Einich, by the crags at the head of the loch.

And so, in thick mist and a mild rain we crept round steaming ledges, burdened by our heavy packs and continually conscious of the approaching night. At length we reached the top of a treacherous chimney that seemed to lead down into the upper reaches of the Glen. Tentatively I climbed down it for a distance of about fifteen feet, matching my weight in reckless abandon against thin stalks of heather and small ledges, but gave it up and returned to James.

"I don't like it" I said bluntly.

"Shall we have to climb again?"

"Yes. If we wait much longer it will be too dark to move."

Dejectedly we retraced our steps. The wind began to blow more strongly and every now and again we caught a glimpse of the loch, a spectral shape in the gloom far below us. The night was settling around the mountain. Great streaming pillars of rock rose above our heads and despite the perilous nature of our position we could not remain unimpressed by the massive natural sculpturing of the place.

Rather fortunately for both of us, we reached that condition of mental apathy in which the body, tired though it be, carries out the commands of the brain with the minimum of complaint or rather, the brain ceases to bother at all and the body works of its own accord.

In the end we mounted the summit of the cliffs, carried out a traverse in the gloom, and went down an easy slope to the loch as fast as conditions allowed. Here, with the prospect of shelter in the Upper Bothy not two miles away, we regained a little optimism. The waters of the loch, mysterious in the twilight, rippled like oil beside us.

When we reached the Bothy... there was no Bothy! Something, or someone, had demolished it. There was not a stone standing, not a coherent shape left to us. The chimney lay shattered on the dripping heather.

We looked at each other and said not a word, and presently, actuated by the hope of the Lower Bothy two miles away, we picked up our packs and set off once again.

The track was trenched with rivulets. Now and then we stumbled for there was very little light left to us, while the wind waved the grasses and the rain fell in a solid deluge.

During those two miles hope fought a losing battle with despair which whispered to us that both Bothies had shared a similiar fate: until we reached a point from whence, even in the gloom, we should have seen the little building.

The familiar outline was absent, yet as we reached it we saw that the destruction of the lower bothy was not as complete as its fellow's had been. The chimney still stood and as we sat dejectedly on a mound of rubble Jimmy said: "We can make a kind of shelter with those bits of corrugated iron up against the chimney, then we'll make a fire."

"Bet the matches are wet," I said gloomily.

But, sure enough, within half an hour, our combined efforts had constructed a tiny water-proof lean-to, and Jimmy had coaxed a splinter of pine root into flame. Our clothes steamed while we brewed tea. At length we grew silent for we were desperately tired and I became a prey to gloomy thoughts and morbid fears. We were but a mile from the spot where Iain and his friend had died.

There were gaps in the walls of our hut where the wooden planks fell short of one another and, despite the warmth of the fire, I shivered and huddled towards it. For a moment the wind ceased and a silence, terrible by contrast, followed. My ears began to appreciate strange sounds. The stream's rushing constancy was most apparent, for the heavy rain had swollen it out of all proportion to its normal size and now and again I fancied that I could hear the rumble of boulders in its bed. Beyond the stream's chorus however, lay a wide range of other sounds, bizarre and misplaced. A little cry came to my ears, an odd fragment of sound, that sent a wave of ice through my spine. I looked at Jimmy but he seemed unaware of it; indeed, I think his thoughts were far away. Suddenly I felt very much alone.

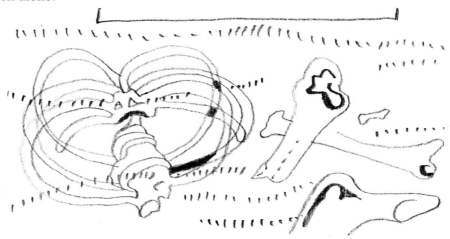

To divert myself I flung more fuel on the fire. The flames licked around it and, having taken a firm hold, leapt up the wide chimney. In my imagination I followed the sparks out into the vacant night, saw them caught by the wind and carried on its turbulent strength up into the vast, stormy air. Then I saw them die out at the foot of the crag where Iain's young strength had failed. Trying to forget this, I looked hard into the heart of the fire where the flames burnt like stars and an image confronted me: a man of fire carried a charred fragment of wood on his back: the Inferno of Dante!

In my mind, the night had assumed the physical shape and psychic significance of an enemy that closed in upon the little patch of fire and light, and human consciousness. This Night to me became a detached personality, the instigator of a vast and terrible process that went on inhumanly. I was horrified by the sense of entire rejection.

The wind rushed past, sucking at the shelter, it lashed the water of the stream against our makeshift structure and my thoughts forsook wholesome reason and raced away on black fantasy aware, as I thought, of some psychic danger, which kept me in a state of exhausted animation.

Time went by on leaden feet. Our shelter groaned with every blast of wind while the fire merely flickered as we fed it the scarce and hard-won fuel. An abstract presence began to grow outside the cone of light, though if Jimmy was aware of it he made no mention; nodding by the fire his only comments were upon the strength of his structure. Although I tried to dismiss it, a conviction seized me that something was waiting for me outside which I felt compelled to face, and so told Jimmy that I would hunt for planks for the fire. Bustled by the wind I walked round for a bit and picked up what I could find in the darkness, yet no one, no thing, was there. When I felt more normal I went back inside.

Then the wind began to blow anew, with a terrible fury and now there was a sense of purpose in it. The Night had discovered us. The mountain fiends were on the rampage. There was evil intent in the elemental pandemonium. Jimmy, glancing at his watch, remarked: "That's a rough day over. It's now midnight."

But the new day came surging up the valley on the wings of a witch's wind. For a moment it was utterly calm, then, as though filled with fresh energy by its brief stillness, it hit the chimney, lifted the corrugated sheets, threw down the supporting planks and with a howl of derision swept on and over the headwall of the glen. Fanned by its furious breath the fire sprang up in sympathy and revealed a lithe figure poised upon the ruins of the bothy walls—so clear was the image in the firelight's blaze, so familiar the features, so true to life the attitude of taut energy seemed this spectre of my dead friend! Then the fire died and with a sense of deep sadness I saw the creation of my overstressed mind vanish.

We roughly reconstructed the lean-to and huddled once more round the fire. Deeply disturbed and shaking with cold I became more and more nervous and depressed and the thought of death began to haunt me. The cold peat of Caledonia would preserve my bones, my flesh would take up its proper place in the earth and my spirit would be free to spring upon the hills. Then, suddenly, I was climbing... I was in the chimney up which I had returned to Jimmy on the previous night. Without any effort I was moving quickly upwards, bracing myself against tufts of heather. Near the top the holds ceased. A stretch of smooth black rock remained. I made a wild attempt to scramble up it and fell. Down I went, turning over and over into limitless depths. All the while the sun was shining on me with an intense heat. Then the sun changed into Jimmy's face and I felt him pull my shoulders away from the fire into which I had all but nodded. My heart was pounding and it took me some moments to clear my thoughts. Three hours or so had gone by. Jimmy told me that he had comfortably dozed by placing his sleeping-bag on a corrugated sheet and he offered me the use of it. Gratefully I accepted and within minutes had lapsed into deep unconsciousness.

When I awoke, remarkably refreshed, I was surprised to see that the river which had roared with such resentment during the night had dropped to a mere trickle; the wind was no more than a breeze and the wonderful smell of moist earth came to my nostrils. The five great crags, still in shadow lay like fangs against the swelling cheeks of the hill and I was glad to find that I could look at them with some composure.

But the memories of the night were still vivid. Sgoran Dubh was beautiful enough now but then, although unseen, it had been a prison for my alienated mind. The feeling of black oppression settled upon my brain and the terror-laden atmosphere encircled me once more; a weakness, thick as night, ran down my spine and turned my legs to lead. Again came a frantic need to escape—not from this place, but from my own ego—to break the bonds of present personality and to return through time to my childhood.

I called to Jimmy. He was gathering wood and turned to me with a reassuring smile. "Sleep well?" he asked. "Excellent, thanks!" I told him, "Want any help?"

Since he said he'd go for a walk alone I resolved to visit the scene of the death fall for the first time. The blood began to course in my veins and I felt the old familiar sense of well-being return. It was some distance to the spot and I only knew its approximate position. As I drew nearer, the crag gathered itself above my head, a fierce virile object, the kind of rock that Iain had loved, for he had always preferred open faces. Out of breath, I turned to look behind where the glen lay at my feet, wondrously beautiful, with its morning colours sparkling like jewels in the sun; at this moment came the long-awaited revelation. Iain's strength, his fearlessness, honesty and joy in living were closely integrated into this rich scene. Here, in altered form, were all the best characteristics of a man who had loved both beauty and adventure; in passing he had returned these qualities to their source.

Eventually I reached the place itself, a soaring buttress above a field of great boulders. Here the last brutal scene had been enacted but suprisingly I found myself unmoved by my proximity to it. Death comes to one and all, I thought, and in these weary years of war he was probably spared worse things.

Thus it was, at this place which was both altar and sepulchre, I finally put aside my grief. I raised my mortal hand in a salute to their immortal spirits, turned in my tracks and ran without stopping to the broken bothy and my living friend.

The Finale

And thus it was at the beginning of my story (on New Year's Day 1943,) that the curtains of sleep were drawn aside on that parting note of happy understanding and I awoke to the anti-climatic knowledge of cold feet and a dying fire. Night hung heavily within the room, although the wind had arisen and was blowing the morning up from the distant regions of the eastern sea; but as yet there was not a glint of light behind the frame of the tiny window. For a few moments I lay listening to the rush and scurry of the frightened air, while the fire made the shadows leap on the walls. I could not immediately disassociate this waking scene from my dreaming memory of the lonely storm-tossed bothy; but slowly comprehension rose out of familiar things and I felt reassured. Yet my mind was still confused and conjured up fancies born of the wind and its uneasy rustling in the branches of the mountain ash outside.

In order to banish fantasy and welcome logic as my companion for the remainder of the dark hours I struggled out of bed and crossed the room to the window. A scene of wild and austere beauty was presented to my gaze. I had been wrong in believing that there would be no light in the sky. An old mis-shapen moon had struggled up from behind the hills to cast a cautious and apologetic glow upon the shadowy moorland. At no great distance from the farm I could see by straining my eyes, the uncertain snow-clad outline of the ancient bridge, whose hump was framed against the thicker darkness of the slopes behind it.

In my attempt to establish psychic stability and rid myself of the prolific shapes of imagination I had actually invoked the latter in a vision of a lifeless land lit by the beams of a lifeless planet. The skeleton arms of the lonely ash, so long exiled from its own kind, waved to the invisible ghost of a vanished forest and beat upon the house in a frenzy of grief. A dull glint of silver, lacing the vacant acres of snow, showed me where the stream lay like a flash of tenuous moonshine flung carelessly across the hills. Above the moor the undulating contour of the horizon was broken and distant uplands plunged down into a deep, craggy recess, whose sparsely wooded slopes, studded with broken rocks, stood out gauntly against the dark blue of the night sky. Across the precipitous face of this recess a thin veil of gossamer mist started up and wandered away like a lonely man's ghost.

As my eye rested upon this distant scene the moon became hidden behind a cloud—and the whole land, whose frosty eminences and craggy defiles were formerly visible in remarkable detail became a mass of vague and chaotic shadows. In the room the quiet breathing of my two friends was the only sound, but in the rooms beyond the bolted door there was no peace. Straining like a ship against the wind, the whole house, so long deprived of happy sound, seemed to listen avidly for any utterance we might make, and I had a sudden desire to shout and shatter such long-established silence. I felt in the very air a sense of grievance that we, who had brought back a measure of life to the house, should presently depart again and leave it to the old insidious onslaughts of time.

Returning from the window, I collected some sticks—for it had grown very cold—and flung them on the fire and lay down beside it. Though I was still tired by the exertions of the night, sleep was tardy and, once more fantasy took its place.

Again my mind, working with that perverse clarity which is a feature of those moments spent courting oblivion, sprang lightly across the crests of a thousand hills and brought back, with poignant force, a thousand evergreen memories. In the vague shapes framed in the leaping light I saw my friends as we had been only a few years before, standing on the threshold of a great and wonderful series of adventures, young and filled with that infinite capacity for joy which belongs to youth. In the stabbing beams I sensed the mutability of life and in the final failing of the glow, its inevitable end. And with this thought, obeying me as though it were a puppet show, the fire began to dance with a pitiful urgency, fraught with an undercurrent of futile sadness.

A penetrating fear ran through my blood that I might die far from the the hills and valleys where the deep streams ran and in my heart I nearly envied those who had perished by the sword upon the slopes of these very hills and their adjoining glens, less than two hundred years before. They were safe now in the security of bodily dissolution, freed from fear. Death in itself held no terrors for me, for I had felt in the glory of the mountain dawn an intuition that could not be disregarded, and in the quiet evening the sense of a gentle, almost satirical smile. The dull fear left my mind then, and in its place came a growing warmth and pleasant apathy, for I was no longer struggling with sleep. Distantly and strange, I could still hear the wind rushing round the house but now there was the sound of triumph in its voice and I sensed that the dawn was near. In the little glen below the Farm I imagined the creaking and groaning of the pines, their soft persuasive music combining with that of all nature to produce a vast tumultous symphony.

In the fireplace a tiny flame brought me back for a moment to the brink of consciousness where, across the room the shadows were quickly marching. A pine log fell from the fire, its beautiful aroma filling the room.

At last the wind was dying away, bringing the morning on its broad shoulders. The voices in the empty rooms were hushed and still and I seemed to be sinking, relaxing into an eternity of emptiness and peace; yet I rallied my senses and murmered a prayer, a pagan prayer to a deity of strength and beauty, who grants continuation upon curious terms.

"O Unknown God," I whispered, and I felt my words rising above the rafters, above the house and far beyond the dying moon into dark-blue beauty, "always let me love these things—the earth, the trees and above all, the mountains: let them bring me comfort when I am sad, strength when I am weary, and when I die, let me be buried in the bosom of the hills where the spring breezes play; give me the certainty of eternal resumption that I may know that nothing is lost and everything returns. Give me a measure of their strength."

The fire with a last bright flicker was gone and the shadows merged into the general gloom. Across the moorland, grown yet more mysterious beneath the promise of the imminent dawn, the silent mountains slept under a frosty sky and in the house there was silence, darkness and peace.

Richard Frere has lived and worked in the Scottish Highlands for the last fifty years. As a young man he discovered a great love of mountains and wild country which has endured throughout his life, and he remains a respected mountaineer. He has been a regular contributor to *The Scots Magazine* and *The Scotsman*; and his close association with writer and naturalist Gavin Maxwell resulted in his successful book *Maxwell's Ghost (1976)*; other titles include: *Beyond The Highland Line (1984)* and most recently, *Loch Ness (1988)* which has met with high acclaim.

Born in Aberdeen in 1934, Eric Ritchie works as a painter, muralist, and teacher, (he is a former lecturer at Edinburgh College of Art). He has exhibited regularly in Scotland and further afield, notably in *The Diaghilev Exhibition*, Edinburgh and London, and one-man shows at Demarco's and the Scottish Gallery in Edinburgh, the Compass Gallery, Glasgow, and others